101

Reasons to Hate

GEORGE
STEINBRENNER

101
Reasons to Hate
GEORGE
STEINBRENNER

Brandon Toropov

A CITADEL PRESS BOOK
Published by Carol Publishing Group

A Citadel Press Book
Published by Carol Publishing Group
Citadel Press is a registered trademark of Carol Communications, Inc.

Editorial, sales and distribution, and rights and permissions inquiries should be
addressed to Carol Publishing Group, 120 Enterprise Avenue, Secaucus, N.J. 07094.

In Canada: Canadian Manda Group, One Atlantic Avenue, Suite 105, Toronto, Ontario
M6K 3E7

Carol Publishing Group books may be purchased in bulk at special discounts for sales
promotion, fund-raising, or educational purposes. Special editions can be created to
specifications. For details, contact Special Sales Department, Carol Publishing Group,
120 Enterprise Avenue, Secaucus, N.J. 07094.

Illustrations by Zina Saunders

Manufactured in the United States of America
10 9 8 7 6 5 4 3 2 1

Library of Congress Cataloging-in-Publication data.

Toropov, Brandon.
    101 reasons to hate George Steinbrenner / by Brandon Toropov
        p.   cm.
    "A Citadel Press book."
    ISBN 0-8065-1854-5
    1. Steinbrenner, George M. (George Michael), 1930– .
2. Baseball team owners–United States–Biography. 3. Baseball team owners–United
States–Miscellanea. I. Title
GV865.S797T67 1997
338.7'61796357'092–dc21   97-11409
    [B]   CIP

This book is dedicated to Mark Waldstein—an unfailing friend and constant ally in the bewildering business of making sense of big-league baseball at the tail end of the twentieth century.

Contents

Foreword, xv

Preface, xvii

Introduction, xix

101 Reasons to Hate George Steinbrenner, 1

Epilogue—Recalling the Roots of the New Beginning
  (A Satirical Fantasia), 155

Notes, 161

Acknowledgments, 168

101 Reasons to Hate George Steinbrenner

by the numbers, comprising some several chapters
in which

1. George secures his destiny
2. George tells a little white lie
3. Yankee fans are fleeced
4. Revenue is used creatively
5. George attacks paying customers
6. George offers anonymous tips
7. George gives a halftime speech
8. George plays favorites
9. George is reported to offer fashion advice
10. Don Mattingly's locks cause a major media event
11. Players receive medical attention
12. George consorts with a scumball
13. The Yankees make a mockery of the term *farm system*
14. George becomes famous for all the wrong reasons
15. A seasoned baseball veteran decides he's had enough
16. It is reported that George forgets a pesky tradition or two
17. George shows concern about his players' fitness

18. George shows concern about his players' vision
19. George dumps on Mr. Strawberry
20. George changes his mind

. . . and in which

21. George engages in transactions of dubious propriety
22. George talks about the family business
23. George ponders New Jersey
24. George berates the Knights of the Keyboard
25. George mouths off
26. George mouths off some more
27. George mouths off some more
28. George mouths off some more
29. George soothes a disgruntled player
30. George has a run-in with his starting catcher
31. George is unclear on the whole Florida concept
32. George shows up his whole pennant-winning team
33. George banishes Graig Nettles
34. George barges in where he's not wanted
35. George barges in where he's not wanted again
36. George has a bad day
37. Thoughtless remarks are tossed around
38. Dave Winfield learns how to spell *revenge:* C-H-A-M-P-I-O-N-S-H-I-P
39. A courtroom squabble goes the Boss's way
40. We learn that two men have more in common than we might want to believe

. . . and in which

41. George hooks up with the single sleaziest individual on the planet
42. George gets the attention he requires
43. George gets some undeserved credit
44. George doesn't
45. Players are insulted in strange ways
46. George takes the direct approach
47. George dumps on non-Yankee employees
48. George spots skullduggery
49. George declines a chance to show his stuff
50. Yearbooks are recalled
51. The Boss holds forth on free agency
52. The Yankee organization muffs a sensitive issue
53. The Yankee organization does it again
54. The Boss disses Gabe Paul
55. The Boss's record at the helm is examined in detail
56. George laughs off a plea to stop the '94 strike
57. George gives some new players a break
58. George's Yankee subordinates face life one grueling day at a time
59. George's Yankee clubhouse staff face life one grueling day at a time
60. George holds forth on trade strategy and makes intimidating noises

. . . and in which

61. George practices an open management style
62. George talks out of both sides of his mouth again

63. George defends New York's honor
64. George has another strange encounter in an elevator
65. George shows that he knows how to make news
66. George botches managerial relations
67. He does it again
68. He does it again
69. He does it again
70. He does it again
71. He does it again
72. He does it again, and this one is a biggie
73. He does it again
74. He does it again
75. He does it again
76. George learns nothing from the 1980s
77. George shows up the manager who least deserved to be shown up
78. Buck and Stick depart
79. Showalter is reported to receive a strange offer
80. George has delusions of grandeur

. . . and in which

81. George has more delusions of grandeur
82. George has more delusions of grandeur
83. George has more delusions of grandeur
84. George has more delusions of grandeur
85. George dismisses Donnie Baseball
86. George dismisses the man he courted so assiduously
87. George whines about how little money he's making

88. George's vocabulary proves that his favorite subject is himself
89. George confiscates equipment
90. George abuses his authority after a tough loss
91. George seeks to infringe his customers' First Amendment rights
92. George makes it up as he goes along
93. George fails to retire gracefully
94. George disses Reggie Jackson
95. Senior front-office officials are stowed behind bushes
96. George gets the holiday spirit
97. George is said to show off his knowledge of the classics
98. A question about the World Championship squad of 1996 is posed
99. George makes a fool of himself on national television
100. We await, with bated breath, the next headline-grabbing fiasco
101. A manager finally talks back to the Boss—and, not long there-after, wins it all

Foreword

Why did I write this book?

Simple. Even though there are probably more than 101 reasons to *love* George Steinbrenner (he is, no kidding, almost certainly one of the most generous people on the face of the earth, and a notable philanthropist whose name is attached to any number of very worthy causes), the man's been tormenting baseball fans for nearly a quarter of a century. Although I have nothing against the man personally and have never met him, I decided to look unflinchingly at the excesses of his regime.

What follows is not, by any stretch of the imagination, everything you need to know about George Steinbrenner. But it is a good chunk of what you need to know about George if you happen to be a long-suffering baseball fan. If you happen to be a long-suffering *Yankees* fan, probably one celebrating the franchise's first world championship since 1978, what follows will help you put things in the proper perspective.

Steinbrenner's team won the World Series in 1996. For that we are grateful. Grateful with the fervent gratitude of a drowning person who has been rescued from the ocean. Deeply grateful. Profoundly grateful. But the victory of the Yankees in the '96 fall classic is not the whole picture for Yankees fans. You know it. I know it. And I think, deep in his heart, George knows it, too.

George is like all of us—he has his good days and his bad days. Many of his bad days, however, have made news . . . and made people wonder what, exactly, he was up to. What follows is not the whole picture, of course, but it is one fan's viewpoint—a viewpoint routinely overlooked, I believe, by the New York Yankees front office.

Let's get started.

—The Author

Preface

Hey. Come on. You didn't buy this book to get all bogged down in this preliminary babbling. Skip the front matter and get to the good stuff.

—The Author

Introduction

What the hell are you doing?

I am sick and tired of people not following *direct orders from the author,* folks. I'm running the show here. I'm the admiral. There may be some vice admirals, but I'm the admiral. So we'd just better not have any more disruptions like this, because it's bad for you, it's bad for me, and, frankly, it's bad for the children of America.

I know there are a couple of readers out there who think I get a little too involved, who think they're better off following their own instincts and playing around with the front matter while the rest of the book is waiting, and waiting, and waiting to be read. If those readers want to play with fire, it's their choice. But let me tell you something about those readers: they may just have a history of insanity in their family, and they may owe everyone in town a whole lot of money, and they may just have long prison records for child molestation and big-time embezzlement.

I'm not naming any names. But I think you people know who you are.

This stuff doesn't have to get out. This situation doesn't *have to* get ugly. As long as we don't have any more of this stupid, stupid insubordination.

Don't you look at me like that. Nobody looks at me like that.

This is *my project*, dammit. I write the forewords around here. I write the prefaces around here. I write the introductions around here. I get to say whether or not people read them. I'm the one calling the shots. If you don't move on to the main part of the book *right now*, there are going to be *serious consequences*, you hear?

And don't go around telling people I'm some kind of *jerk*, either. You knew exactly what you were getting into when you picked this book up. You didn't have to start reading it. But you did.

Act *rationally*, for God's sake.

You are *still reading this introduction*, you moron. What are you, nuts? All right. Just for that, I *forbid* you to read the rest of this book. Don't you even try.

You hear me?

—*The Author*

101
Reasons to Hate
GEORGE
STEINBRENNER

"Hey, it's [Steinbrenner's] team. But we have our turf, too. . . . When all else fails, we can use our ultimate weapon. We can quote him."
    —*Murray Chass*

1. In the Beginning . . .

The early seventies: The Steinbrenner era begins as the Cleveland shipbuilder helps to lead a consortium that purchases the Yankees from the CBS television network. The announcement of the change of ownership takes place on January 3, 1973.

The Troubles follow.

Steinbrenner brought to New York a tale of tumult, disorder, and pain. Would it had never commenced—or, failing that, would that it had commenced elsewhere, to less notice and less ill effect.

As it happens, the Boss latched onto the most storied organization in all of sports after having tried, and failed, to purchase the Cleveland Indians franchise. Nothing against Indians fans, of course—their club has now emerged, after a long period of futility, as one of the American League powerhouses of the last decade of the century, but Steinbrenner, boss of the Indians, probably would have been a lot less traumatic for big-league baseball. Steinbrenner, Boss of the Yankees, produced easily twice as many nervous breakdowns and media-driven conniption fits as he would have in Ohio, just because a lot more people were paying attention.

Had George secured the perpetually underachieving Indians club of the early seventies, rather than the high-profile franchise forever associated with Ruth, Gehrig, DiMaggio, and Mantle, it's conceivable that the damage he would have inflicted on the national pastime would have been considerably less. But he didn't. Because of the Yankee organization's history, prestige, and tradition, and because of New York's status as a national and international media center, Steinbrenner found himself on the world's biggest stage, with his name attached to the world's most famous sports franchise.

Baseball people thought life at Yankee Stadium under CBS had been bad. (The team finished dead last in 1966, and fans thought the apocalypse was surely at hand.) They had no idea how *bad* bad could get with Steinbrenner as principal owner.

I hate Steinbrenner . . . for not buying the Cleveland Indians instead.

2. Hands-off Ownership—Cross My Heart and Hope to Die

"I won't be active in the day-to-day operations of the club at all. I can't spread myself too thin. I've got enough headaches with the shipping company."
    —*Steinbrenner's comment at the 1973 news conference announcing CBS's sale of the New York Yankees.*

The Red Sox will someday win the World Series once again. Yoko Ono didn't have anything to do with the breakup of the Beatles. And George Steinbrenner won't be active in the day-to-day operations of the New York Yankees.

All together now: Liar, liar, pants on fire!

3

The Boss's seemingly innocuous assurance marks the beginning of the end of the tradition of stability and professionalism in the once-legendary New York Yankee organization. This deceptively simple-sounding lie is the point at which the Yankees began to earn their status as just another big-league baseball team, and this one led by a man thoroughly capable of mediocrity, sordid meddling from the top, epically lousy people skills, still lousier decision making, and generally incompetent self-aggrandizement. Steinbrenner may have three world championships to point to, championships that came after he made his now laughable statement about playing a no-interference role as owner. He also has a legacy of chaos, dishonesty, mismanagement, and seemingly limitless petulance that reaches far further than the memory of the seasons of 1977, 1978, and, yes, 1996 will ever extend. With this promise, the Steinbrenner regime is on display in all its mentality.

In the gentle, businesslike cadences of this, the very first Steinbrenner lie of the Yankee era, the initial sounds of the perversion of a proud dynasty can be very, very faintly made out in the distance. It's a sad sound indeed. Who can say what past and future heartaches and disgraces could have been avoided if Steinbrenner had kept his word after making this vow? As it stands, the Boss blindsided Yankee fans—and not for the last time, either.

Sure, there's an upside. Repeated exposure to the stressful situations arising out of Steinbrenner's many deceptions may have built some character and endurance among legions of Yankees fans. But did we have to have this man on board for a quarter century in order to make such progress?

Steinbrenner would later lie about having told this lie. Would you have expected anything less?

I hate Steinbrenner . . . for this, the first and perhaps most devastating Big Lie of his reign.

3. Tickets, Please

"GORGE US GEORGE: The Boss raises Yanks' top ticket by 47 percent"
   —*November 2, 1994,* New York Post *headline reporting Yankee move hiking the cost of lower box seats between the dugouts and some loge seats from seventeen to twenty-five dollars. A Yankee spokesperson defended the move as an attempt to "identify a premier seating area of the stadium."*

Did you notice the timing here? *While baseball fans are fuming about the first postponed World Series since 1904,* the Yankees decide to "identify premier seating area[s]." Talk about a move unlikely to win over the goodwill of paying customers. This man has chutzpah the likes of which mortal man has never seen.

The motivation? Who knows? Separation of (justifiably furious) Yankees fans from their hard-earned cash sure seems like a bit of a stretch, doesn't it? We know *that* motivation didn't play any part in this incident. Maybe, what with the strike and all, he was hoping to reinforce the importance of comic timing.

Just in case you're keeping score at home, the papers recently reported that the Yankees announced *another* ticket increase—this one running a hefty 29 percent—after winning the 1996 World Series. No, it's not your imagination. George is getting away with what he can get away with, while he can get away with it. Again.

Yep. These prices are going up considerably faster than the standard of living in the economy as a whole. That's because there's a simple two-step formula at work: If the recent news is bad, raise the ticket prices. And if the recent news is good, raise the ticket prices.

I hate Steinbrenner . . . for his unconscionable ticket price hikes.

4. Help Me If You Can, My Shipping Business Is Hurting . . .

"General Manager Gene Michael . . . asserted during the 1992 season that the Yankees didn't have enough money to go after the free agents that he wanted. The reason that they didn't, as it turned out, was that they had been borrowing heavily against an unprecedented $486 million contract with the cable Madison Square Garden (MSG) network and WABC radio to distribute profits to team partners and to help Steinbrenner bail out his ailing shipbuilding company."

   —*Still more unsettling news for Yankees fans. Michael eventually distanced himself from his reported remarks.*

Sure. He's the principal owner. He can do what he wants with his own money. Business is business. Nobody can make him treat one operation more like the national pastime than another.

It still stank to high heaven.

I hate Steinbrenner . . . because his commitment to the New York Yankees sometimes takes a distinct backseat to his other business concerns.

5. Ripping New York Yankees Fans

Want to hear George Steinbrenner's assessment of his own paying customers? "Our people in New York have been a big disappointment in support of this team." That's how the Boss was quoted in the September 29, 1996 *New York Times*. Dark aspersions on the moral fibers of players, Yankee executives and members of the media are not enough. The man wants to be sure to let the people who *pass through the turnstiles* know that they're not quite measuring up either.

If memory serves, not even the dictatorial Charles O. Finley sank this low. Finley faced serious attendance problems while fretting and fuming over an Oakland A's club that snagged three straight World Championships in the seventies. He pulled just about every self-serving trick in the book: threatening to move the team, berating the press, mouthing off to his players, and second-guessing his managers. (He was, as you can see, a kind of proto-Boss.) Finley also launched opportunistic promotions—such as the comely "ball girls" meant to add a dash of sex appeal to a night at the old ballpark. But dissing the fans? Even Finley realized that wouldn't put any more fannies in the seats.

This may sound like an innocuous slip of the tongue, but in an era when fans are content to dismiss wealthy players *and* wealthy owners with a weary roll of the eyes, such attacks make about as much sense as, oh, raising ticket prices right after a prolonged strike that cost baseball a World Series.

I hate Steinbrenner . . . because his own unique brand of naive self-absorption leads him to believe he can get away with lecturing the people who make the National Pastime possible at the big-league level in the first place. The fans.

6. **A Highly Placed Source Within the Yankee Organization—One With Lousy People Skills, a Habit of Berating Everyone in Sight, and a Tendency Toward Complete Self-Absorption—Has Revealed on a Confidential Basis That . . .**

Steinbrenner's bias is usually so obvious that the ruse of offering himself up as a "highly placed source" is usually transparent to sports fans. Sometimes the Boss has been known to forget what's meant to be attributed to him and what isn't, with the intriguing result that Sportswriter A writes a story attributing a remark to a highly placed

Yankee source, while Sportswriter B writes a story attributing a virtually identical remark to Steinbrenner.

It keeps things interesting.

I hate Steinbrenner . . . for his clumsy, heavy-handed, and uniformly self-serving attempts at anonymous media manipulation.

7. Look at Me, I'm Knute Rockne

"Well fellas, this is it—the big game."

Vince Lombardi had a way with words like that. The Boss would love to have a way with words like that. But let's face it, the Boss does not have a way with words like that.

The whole pep-talk-before-the-big-showdown thing really doesn't seem to be George's genre. But for some reason, though, known only to him, he's made more than his share of them.

Steinbrenner's demotivating motivational locker-room speeches have left some players shaking their heads in amazement, some staring blankly into space, and some wondering which sport the owner thinks he's involved in. One thing these exhortations usually haven't done, though, is get players pumped up and thinking about winning.

These lectures have never, ever had the effect George seems to think they're going to have. So suppose we leave the half-time speeches to the football coaches . . . and let the baseball manager handle mental-focus issues with the players? All in favor please signify by saying "aye." The motion is approved.

I hate Steinbrenner . . . for the idiotic locker-room pep talks that leave no one but George feeling good.

8. Will Everyone Who's Sick of Hearing Robert Merrill Sing "The Star Spangled Banner" Please Take One Step Forward?

Why is this man still singing the national anthem before Yankee games? Isn't there some aria from a famous Italian opera whose title translates as "Get Me Out of Here, I'm Washed Up"? Perhaps he could sing that once or twice, privately and in the Boss's quarters, for a little change of pace.

Did anyone else besides me notice that Merrill flubbed up the lyrics of "The Star Spangled Banner" during the 1996 World Series? This man has now sung this song approximately four hundred million times before Yankees games. I know it was a high-pressure situation, but isn't it *possible* that Merrill has been doing this for a little too long?

I hate Steinbrenner . . . for massively overestimating Merrill's talents and for virtually turning him into a fixture as part of a predictable (and traumatic) pregame ritual at Yankee Stadium.

9. We'll Have No Slovenliness on This Team, Buddy

According to Robert Obojski's book *Baseball's Strangest Moments*, the story is told that, during one Yankee spring training session in Florida, Steinbrenner instructed a player to wear his cap properly by turning it around bill front. The player in question was, we are told, a catcher, preparing to play defense.

Apparently, George runs a very tight ship, folks. There will be none of this turning-your-cap-around nonsense, no matter *what* position you play. Is that understood?

If the story is accurate, it opens the door to a host of future Steinbrenner-inspired trends in on-field dress and grooming. George may yet decide to inform outfielders that they must wash their faces of the unattractive, strangely symmetrical black streaks beneath the eyes that so often mar their appearance, or to order batters not to don form-fitting gloves at the plate unless they intend to supply enough pairs for the defensive team to wear as well.

Don't get me started about haircuts.

I hate Steinbrenner . . . for trying, on any number of occasions, to establish dominance he hasn't earned by telling people how they ought to look and dress—when he'd be far better off keeping his mouth shut.

10. Hair Today, Gone Tomorrow

"The Case of Oscar Gamble . . . happened in spring training about fifteen years ago. Gamble was a new Yankee outfielder whose hair style was such that he wore his baseball hat about two feet over his head. The Yankees refused to give him a uniform until he had his Afro felled."
    —*Ira Berkow reminisces about a Yankee front-office "statement" from days gone by.*

"During the 1977 season, Thurman Munson, angry with Steinbrenner, defied club rules and grew a beard during a road trip. . . . Munson eventually shaved in a motel room in Syracuse, where the team was playing an exhibition game."
    —*Murray Chass on another reminder that the much ballyhooed Mattingly haircut controversy was not the first of the Steinbrenner regime.*

"Don Mattingly refuses to get a haircut and the Yankees swoop down on him like the secret police. They want action. They want Mattingly to meet a pair of scissors."
    —*Jack Curry on the benching and fining of the Yankees star who refused to get his hair cut. Eventually, Mattingly gave in and clipped his locks.*

"The Steinbrenner influence lives."
    —*Murray Chass appears to sense the ominous, nay, otherwordly power of the banished owner during the Mattingly crisis.*

I told you not to get me started about haircuts.

Don Mattingly deserves the Congressional Medal of Honor, the Croix de Guerre, and any and all dollars he has managed to wring from the Boss over the course of his distinguished playing career (or afterward, for that matter). Why? He at least attempted to draw the line here.

Steinbrenner—in exile at the time of the Mattingly conflict, but presumably in full accord with the long-established company line—is apparently really *bugged* by long hair. It's as if persistent denial and large amounts of cash could mean the sixties never occurred. The lesson for today, boys and girls, is a simple one: possession first. All else second. Those who possess set the standards. If you write the check, you get to see the neck.

No, these events weren't the Black Sox scandal. Yes, the hair flap does reflect something dangerously and fundamentally wrong: a style of dealing with people based on the idea that you, um, own them. That notion is pure George, and it's one of his most unwelcome legacies to the game of baseball. The Boss doesn't "own" players, or former players, or the fans, or the press, but somehow this update seems to have slipped past him.

This whole "ownership" worldview plainly stinks, not to put too fine a point on the matter, and it is the source of much that has been fatally askew with the sport in general, and the Yankees in particular, during the last quarter of this century. The haircut episode may *sound* like no particular big deal in the grand scheme of things, but it is (no kidding) the whole Steinbrenner problem in microcosm, because it illustrates all that is dark and misguided and, yes, now and then even disconcertingly sulfuric about the Boss.

This whole pattern of dictatorial grandstanding carries ominous consequences, in the author's view, for baseball as an institution. Don't laugh. The "I own you *and* your hair" outlook is proof that we still have to deal with owners who haven't got a clue about human autonomy, despite their unlikely mutterings about Abraham Lincoln (on whom the Boss may at any moment—you stand forewarned—begin discoursing at length).

I hate Steinbrenner . . . for the whole slaveholder mentality—a mentality that is out of place, and then some, in the last decade of the twentieth century.

11. Doctor, Doctor, Give Me the News

Not-exactly-a-sign-of-trust-from-the-top department: "[In 1982] Steinbrenner issue[d] a statement ordering Doyle Alexander to undergo a physical, adding that he feared for the safety of the players behind the pitcher."

Some people think the sports media exist to keep people informed about how the local team is performing on the field. The Boss knows better. The sports media exist in order to provide the principal owner with a convenient way of establishing dominance over players, managers, and front-office personnel through personal humiliation.

It's hard to keep track of exactly how many times George has pulled this nifty trick. The principal smear campaigns of the Steinbrenner era are detailed within these covers, but there are certainly more examples of this pattern than this book can outline. Alexander's case was one of the most fascinating, in that the Boss attempted to appeal to the moral authority of the medical establishment in the public humiliate-the-player routine. It's a little bit like using a skywriting service to tell your kid that since he got a C on his test instead of an A, he'll have to get a shot from that nurse he really hates.

As an isolated incident, the public attack on Alexander isn't even one of the Boss's more imaginative maneuvers. As an example of Steinbrenner's disturbing habit of using the media as his own means of settling scores and acting on misplaced grudges, however, it does have one common element with the other look-what-I-can-say-about-you-in-the-papers escapades. It backfired.

Surprise, surprise. Alexander didn't perform well in pinstripes; the Yankees traded him the following season. As a member of the Toronto Blue Jays, however, the pitcher turned things around. In 1983 he led the American League in winning percentage. Too bad he didn't get the chance to perform at the top of his game while he was a Yankee.

What, you may ask, is the prescription for fans who put up with an owner who pulls this sort of nonsense? Take two banishments from the game of baseball and call me in the morning. And you're going to *need* to call me in the morning, because that pesky George virus is going to be back.

I hate Steinbrenner . . . because Alexander, like so many others, was intimidated and humiliated into performing at subpar levels while he played for the New York Yankees.

12. Can You Say "Howiegate"?

"The battle between player and owner focused on the Winfield Foundation, which Steinbrenner refused to fund until what he considered financial irregularities had been straightened out. . . . [An] investigation by Fay Vincent's office [in 1990] revealed that Steinbrenner had, two years earlier, paid Howard Spira, a professional gambler and a one-time employee of the foundation, $40,000 to provide information damaging to Winfield."

How bad was Howiegate? This sordid affair actually put a story that *should* have been front-page news—the Yankees' worst season in nearly seven decades—on the back burner. In 1990 it became clear that Steinbrenner had consorted with Spira and paid him forty thousand dollars. The press had a field day, the fans had yet another reason to boo the Boss, and Fay Vincent had a reason to draw a line in the sand.

Not surprisingly, Steinbrenner didn't take his Howie-inspired expulsion from the game at all well (the wording wasn't to his liking), and fans were treated to another of his media-enhanced tirades. With a characteristic lack of restraint, Steinbrenner called Commissioner Fay Vincent a liar, and expressed his doubts as to Vincent's ability to "serve as commissioner and to act rationally." Fans asked themselves whose capacity for rational action was really at issue.

Paying sleazeballs to keep an ear out for bad news about your own ballplayers isn't *quite* as bad as, say, the 1994 strike, but it's pretty bad. Some have tried to paint Steinbrenner, rather than the long-term interests of the game, as the biggest victim in this tawdry episode. The boss's defenders have probably been vacationing in another dimension. Howie was a four-star lowlife. That George had anything whatsoever to do with his dirt-dishing is inexcusable. He didn't *have* to keep taking the man's calls. He didn't have to extend his networking efforts into the gutter. But he did. And he got in over his head.

File this one under Wages of Utter Paranoia. Steinbrenner should never have encouraged any relationship with Spira, period. The senseless rivalry the Boss initiated with Dave Winfield—of which Howiegate was only the culmination—represents a conduct low, even for the Boss.

Further examples of Steinbrenner's eerily irrational feud with his star outfielder can be found elsewhere in this book—but none of them tops this fiasco.

Steinbrenner came back from the dead, of course. He'd had practice with this sort of thing. (The skinny on Steinbrenner's *first* commissioner-mandated separation from the game is discussed elsewhere in this volume.) Fay Vincent himself exited, yielding to an "acting commissioner" arrangement that seems unlikely to produce anyone who will hold the Boss accountable for the consequences of his various paranoid fantasies anytime in the near future.

I hate Steinbrenner . . . for consorting with Howie Spira, and for wriggling his way back into big-league baseball after the commissioner's office had been sufficiently weakened for him to do so.

13. Space Shot: The Columbus Shuttle

THE BOSS WATCH

"Beattie was scared stiff. What the hell was he doing out there?"
   —*Steinbrenner's public assessment of Yankee pitcher Jim Beattie,*
      shortly before the latter was shipped to the minor leagues in 1978.

"You say you can't tell from one outing? The hell you can't."
   —*Steinbrenner's curt assessment of the performance of pitcher Mike*
      Griffin during a spring training game. Griffin was demoted to
      Columbus the next day.

"Columbus, here I come."
   —*Steinbrenner on pitcher Dennis Rasmussen in 1986, who ended up*
      evading the Shuttle and actually led the team with 18 victories that
      year.

As humbling an experience as it must be for big-leaguers, getting sent to the minors at some point in one's career is usually part of the game. Any number of players, however, have found that being sent to the minors during the most chaotic period of George Steinbrenner's stewardship of the New York Yankees could be hazardous to your career.

Prospects Scott Nielsen and Ken Clay, among many others, were subjected to high-profile abuse thanks to Steinbrenner's Shuttle system, a morale-shattering rapid transit arrangement if there ever was one. At its worst the Shuttle reflected the ever-shifting priorities at the top of the Yankee organization more than any realistic assessment of player potential. Countless careers suffered as a result of Steinbrenner's world-famous snap decisions.

The Columbus Shuttle allowed Steinbrenner to find new and exciting ways to use his authority to punish incompetence—as he defined it. Steinbrenner publicly ripped pitcher Jim Beattie (previous page) after a defeat at the hands of the Boston Red Sox endured by the Yankee hurler and in a stormy phone call, ordered coach Gene Michael to "get rid of him." Pitcher Dave LaRoche made a total of four round trips between New York and Columbus in 1982. In 1984 shortstop Bobby Meacham was dispatched to the minors when he made an error in the fourth game of the season. At one point Meacham earned the honor of being the Yankees' twenty-first shortstop over a ten-year period.

Sometimes it was the decision to bring people in *from* the minor leagues that caused problems. Jose Rijo, whose too-early arrival in the big leagues may have all but guaranteed that he'd have trouble with the Boss, falls into this category. Catcher Juan Espino may have scored the ultimate Shuttle-related coup when he was summoned from Columbus during the 1982 season and then ordered to return *before he even had the chance to suit up for a single game.*

The shambles that the Yankee farm "system" became probably cost the game more than a few promising careers. Steinbrenner was responsible for this travesty.

I hate Steinbrenner . . . for the Columbus Shuttle and its attendant personnel chaos.

14. How to Become a Household Name

Easy. Own the New York Yankees and lie a whole lot for about a quarter of a century.

"[There are] statements I believed were true when I made them." That's how Steinbrenner was quoted in the August 6, 1990 issue of *Newsweek,* dismissing talk of "lies." Other people have had different views of the Boss's veracity.

Chicago White Sox coowner Jerry Reinsdorf once said, "I know how to tell when George Steinbrenner is lying. His lips move." His 1983 barb at the Yankees' principal owner is one of the most-quoted assessments of the Boss's creative attitude toward real-world accountability for spoken promises, but it's certainly not the only one.

Catfish Hunter weighed in with the following: "He's a man of his word, even though a lot of times you have to get it in writing to make sure of it."

Then there's star pitcher Jack Morris's recollection of Steinbrenner's pained decision not to make a more competitive offer to Morris in 1985, during the Long National Nightmare That Was Later

Determined to Be Collusion: "Steinbrenner said no one told him what to do. In fact, he swore on his mother's name about it. All I can say now is, 'Poor Mom.'"

For better or for worse, it appears that lying (or, if you prefer, making statements that turn out not to be true here on planet earth) has earned Steinbrenner some great one-liners—and perhaps just as much attention and press as his legendary people skills and the role his celebrated free spending played in ushering in the Era of Free Agency.

This is what America is all about, kids. Growing up wealthy, using money to control people, and then, most important of all, talking off the top of your head, without regard for whether or not what you have to say is accurate or fair. That's how you earn a lot of headlines and that coveted "oh, look, there goes so-and-so" status as you walk down the street.

How does that James Taylor song go? "I was only telling a lie." Pretty much standard operating procedure for the Boss. Stop the presses! He may be telling another one!

I hate Steinbrenner . . . because he's become famous for all the wrong reasons.

15. Badgering Al Rosen Until He Quit

"Al [Rosen] was a good man who tried to be a good president of the club. He was. He just couldn't take being subservient to the man [Steinbrenner]. He had pride. He had done things in this

game. What George has done to him is terrible. George just thinks
he can buy everybody. Some guys have pride. You can't buy them."
  —*Reggie Jackson on Al Rosen's 1979 resignation as Yankee president.*

Hey, we shouldn't complain too much. He could have *fired* Rosen,
rather than merely hounding him constantly, and thus inspiring him
to resign.

Rosen, a standout third baseman on the memorable Cleveland
Indians teams of the forties and fifties, was an effective, capable baseball executive who had endured one too many soul-sapping conflicts
with George Steinbrenner. Like manager Ralph Houk, another consummate pro, Rosen ultimately decided that the best way to work
with the Boss was to stop trying and just leave the organization. The
Yankees would have been a lot better off if it had been the owner
who left the team for good.

Rosen moved on to greener pastures and was no doubt glad to
have been able to do so.

I hate Steinbrenner . . . because his dysfunctional organization has mis-
treated—and consumed—an entire collection of intelligent, experienced,
and accomplished baseball men by granting them only nominal control.

16. Oh? What Rule Is That?

"[Billy] Martin never discouraged stories that made Steinbrenner
appear ignorant of baseball's niceties. One such story was that . . .

[once] when the Yankees had a runner on third base with two out, and the batter hit a slow ground ball to shortstop, and the runner on third crossed home plate before the batter was thrown out at first base, Steinbrenner stood and cheered, believing wrongly that the run counted."

This is an oft-recited story assigned to Steinbrenner's early years as Yankee boss. Whether or not it actually happened is hard to say, since Martin did spin his share of tall tales and was certainly a man who had his vindictive moments. If the "applause" story is true, the incident takes its place among any number of other "amateurish baseball" episodes generally attributed to the Boss.

Hey. He *could* have asked Martin why they sometimes don't play the home half of the ninth inning. But he didn't.

I don't think.

I hate Steinbrenner . . . because he was barking orders to men who had been in and around organized baseball for most of their adult lives while he was enrolled in Baseball 101.

17. Weighty Matters

Here's Steinbrenner's 1982 rationalization for leaking word to the press that Piniella's contract featured a clause under which the player could be fined one thousand dollars for every pound over two hundred he weighed: "Sometimes Lou has to be treated like a nineteen-year-old. Everybody in Tampa [Piniella's home town] will tell you that. He knew what he was signing."

Word of Piniella's fines reached the tabloids before they reached the Yankee outfielder. A particularly innovative humiliate-the-player-via-the-media move, yes?

Piniella appears to have put up with more grief from the Boss than all but a select few individuals. He's up there with Berra and Martin in terms of pure outrageousness endured from the Boss. This excess-pounds flap may have been the low point of Piniella's relationship with Steinbrenner while serving as an active player (though further horrors awaited him as a manager and Yankee executive). Third baseman Graig Nettles, who was also publicly criticized about his weight by Steinbrenner, observed that Steinbrenner's lack of expertise in the area of baseball was exceeded only by his lack of expertise in the area of weight control.

I hate Steinbrenner . . . because he often comes on way, way, way too heavy.

18. I Can See Clearly Now

"Reggie [Jackson] was having a bad year. His timing was off, he was striking out a lot, he stayed in one of his funks. And Steinbrenner was dogging him in the papers, making him go for eye tests."

—*Dave Winfield recalls one more touching example of the Boss's concern for a player's welfare.*

As we have seen, he pulled the same type of stunt with pitcher Doyle Alexander. Classy, huh?

But let's not jump to conclusions. This whole eye-exam business doesn't *necessarily* mean the Boss was trying to show Jackson up by ripping him in the merciless New York City tabloids. His aim wasn't *necessarily* to watch the *New York Post* grind Jackson to a fine paste in the next morning's edition. Steinbrenner may have been eager to make a national statement on behalf of optometrists to promote the importance of regular eye exams. Who knows what was going through George's mind? Steinbrenner may have been trying to send Reggie a subtle metaphorical message about taking a long view of things and keeping his slump in perspective.

Then again, maybe he was trying to show Jackson up.

If there were a market for *anti*motivational specialists, people who knew exactly how to get all the members of a team utterly depressed, sniping at one another, falling short of their goals, and pulling in completely different directions, George would be the king of the hill. You'd see him on the cover of *Success* magazine six times a year. When you turned on the television at two in the morning, you'd see his infomercial offering a series of you-too-can-under-achieve audiocassettes.

I hate Steinbrenner . . . because he sometimes seems to live for the pleasure of making other people feel bad about themselves—*especially* people who have the potential to emerge as leaders in the Yankee clubhouse.

19. Lest You Think the Boss's Ability to Badmouth His Own Players Would Pass After His Costly Vendetta Against Dave Winfield, After Which You'd *Think* He'd Have Learned Something . . .

"Giving him a chance to revive his baseball career is better than having a thirty-three-year-old junkpile on the street."
   —*Steinbrenner's reported assessment of newly signed Yankee Darryl Strawberry.*

Good thing the Boss hasn't lost the personal touch after all these years, eh? Nothing like a warm welcome to the team from the pastime's most celebrated "people person," I always say.

Old ways die hard, and talking other people down—particularly athletes who draw lots of headlines—is one of the oldest tricks in Steinbrenner's bag.

Yes, it was great that he gave Strawberry a shot that ultimately resulted in key contributions to a world championship team. *No,* Steinbrenner may never learn to stop denigrating others when he's within range of a notebook or a microphone.

File this one under "convincing proof that old dogs really don't learn new tricks." If the Boss is still reverting to character assassination as a reflex reaction (Howie Spira, why did we not heed your significance?), and if Steinbrenner is still in baseball in, say, the year 2005, the game as a whole deserves everything that befalls it for not getting rid of the Boss.

I hate Steinbrenner . . . because he can make even a classy personnel move like signing Darryl Strawberry look cheap, tawdry, and mean-spirited.

20. The Fine Art of Switching Positions on Players One Has Humiliated in the Press

"Definitely fat and probably finished."
>   —*Steinbrenner's 1980 assessment of third baseman Graig Nettles. Nettles was far from finished: He played until 1983 in New York and was a starter on the 1984 San Diego Padres squad that made it to the World Series.*

"I'd take him back anytime."
>   —*Steinbrenner in 1989 on Graig Nettles.*

▼

"Reggie isn't doing the job. I don't know what's wrong with him."
>   —*Steinbrenner during the 1980 pennant race, using the press to put some pressure on Reggie Jackson. On another occasion, Steinbrenner won headlines and humiliated his slugger by expressing grave public*

doubts about the soundness of Jackson's vision. Mr. October was soon off to California.

"[Dave] Winfield's a good athlete, but he's no Reggie."
  —*Steinbrenner to the press early in 1982. Apparently a dyed-in-the-wool Reggie Jackson fan, George lets loose on his latest enemy.*

▼

"Mr. May."
  —*Steinbrenner's notorious assessment of star outfielder Dave Winfield.*

"No Takers for Overpriced Winfield, Says Boss."
  —*Headline from an August 1986* New York Post *story in which Stein-brenner trotted out statistics in order to show just how hard it would be to trade Winfield. Not exactly a vote of confidence from the top.*

"Everything was going so well, and then along he comes with this book."
  —*Winfield teams up with Tom Parker to write* Winfield: A Player's Life, *which was, er, not uniformly flattering to the Yankee boss. Thus a puzzled, persecuted Boss ponders his betrayal at the hands of the outfielder-turned-bestselling-author. What on earth could have caused Winfield to turn on George in such a public way?*

In recent years, Steinbrenner has been quick to argue that "the media" is responsible for his less than perfect public image. If only the unrelenting, headline-hungry bad boys in the press room would stop *hounding* him, he seems to be saying, people would get the chance to see him for the straight shooter he really is.

It might make sense—in an alternate universe—if George's record of attempted media manipulation didn't keep blinking on and off for attention like a neon sign in a bad detective movie. Here's the Boss's time-tested plan: Use intentionally generated bad press to pursue rivalries (typically, *pointless* rivalries) and then compare *today's* bad guy with *yesterday's* bad guy, who is now today's *good* guy. Leaving aside for the moment the fact that this strategy is just a *little* Orwellian, the idea that there's some plot on the part of the national media because they point out the Boss's jaw-dropping inconsistencies just won't stand up. Turnarounds like the ones listed on the preceding page have a way of convincing a lot of print and broadcast people that the Boss deserves every hole in the floor he finds himself standing over. And you know what? They're right.

Steinbrenner often seems to *need* someone to face off against—hard and in a very public way—and he doesn't mind trashing reputations or flatly contradicting himself while he's on the offensive. God help you if you're caught in his sights. But even if you are, you can take comfort in the fact that he'll probably be praising you to the skies when it's time to launch a guided front-page missile in someone else's direction.

By the way, George is very often proven quite ludicrously *wrong* about the people he's decided to trash in public. Nettles was a big part of the San Diego Padre National League flag in 1984; Jackson finished the 1980 season with 41 home runs and a .300 batting average; Reggie was eventually elected to the Hall of Fame and assumed a job (who knows why—see entry 69) with the Yankees; Winfield wrapped up 1986 having knocked in 100 or more runs for the fifth straight year and was a 1992 postseason star for the Toronto Blue Jays.

I hate Steinbrenner . . . because he talks out of both sides of his mouth about players he's attacked—and thus makes Bill Clinton look like a model of consistency.

21. Funny Money

"It had to do with the violations of a fifty-nine-year-old law that most attorneys didn't even know about during the Nixon campaign. It had to do with corporate donations to his campaign, Richard Nixon's campaign. . . . What I did is I went to my boys and I said, 'Look, if you give a dollar, I'll give three to the campaign.' . . . Many corporations in this country were guilty. . . . I just feel a little differently than a lot of the others who let the number three and four man step in and take the blame."
   —*Steinbrenner's explanation to* Sixty Minutes *of his illegal contributions to the Nixon campaign.*

"Out of the goodness of my heart."
   —*One of Steinbrenner's less convincing explanations for his decision to pay gambler Howie Spira forty thousand dollars.*

Touching, yes?
   Isn't it sad when people get all worked up over one human being trying to help out another? Isn't that a sign of the crazy, mixed-up times in which we live? Doesn't it seem just a *little* cynical to suggest that anything other than the most benevolent motives were

guiding the Yankee boss while he was getting in over his head with a morally challenged, loudmouthed lowlife who claimed to have some good "dish" on a man against whom the Boss nursed a borderline pathological grudge? Doesn't it seem unfair to suggest that he was doing anything other than being completely forthright when he directed his employees to circumvent existing campaign finance laws?

Appeals to his own altruism and accountability did not help Steinbrenner's case with commissioners Bowie Kuhn and Fay Vincent, respectively. His (gasp!) Nixonian stonewalling comeback campaigns, of which these are perhaps the most entertaining excerpts, only added to the surrealistic appeal of the events leading up to George's two heave-hos from the game. We must, as always, give him credit for impeccable comic timing.

The question remains, though: Why would George have believed he could actually *get away* with whoppers like these? Maybe he had the inspiring model of the Master of San Clemente himself in mind.

I hate Steinbrenner . . . for lying about payoffs and bringing the worst kind of hypocrisy to the highest levels of big-league baseball.

22. Meet the New Boss, Same as the Old Boss

"My son Hank, subject to league approvals, will become general partner at this time."
　　—*Steinbrenner statement to the press in August 1990.*

In the event, Hank Steinbrenner didn't take over his father's ball club. After a good deal of chaos, negotiation, and good old-fashioned gridlock saw the departure of Robert Nederlander as general partner and the rejection of attorney Daniel McCarthy, the various parties finally agreed that Steinbrenner's *son-in-law,* Joseph Molloy, could take over as head of the Yankees. In March of 1993 the Boss was back at the helm.

The notion of members of the Boss's immediate family taking over effective control of the team struck many baseball fans in 1990 as odd, especially given the Big Guy's stated decision to remove himself "permanently" from club activities, rather than accept a two-year suspension. (His statement to the press had read, "For some years now, I have been preparing to turn over the operation of the Yankees to my sons and sons-in-law.") *Time* magazine reported that "commissioner [Fay Vincent] guesses that Steinbrenner believed the fig leaf of continuing as a silent partner in the Yankees would allow him to hang on to his other sports post as a vice president of the U.S. Olympic Committee."

For all the occasionally inscrutable machinations surrounding his 1990 departure from the game, including his initial choice to name his son as his successor, Steinbrenner deserves a nice loud round of gleeful raspberries from the fans in the bleachers. For his eventual return to baseball in 1993, he deserves still another round.

By the way, I know how to get Steinbrenner out of baseball for good. Ready? Wait until he's darn well ready to retire. You wait and see. That's the way it will finally happen.

I hate Steinbrenner . . . for the transparent attempts at nepotism that hung like a cloud over his supposedly permanent 1990 banishment from baseball.

23. The Fine Art of Squeezing Cash From State and Municipal Sources by Threatening to Move One's Team

"The battle [between New York and New Jersey over whether key businesses will move] could be a warm-up for a truly titanic struggle over the Yankees. While New Jersey has not yet made a public offer to owner George Steinbrenner, it reportedly has been preparing a proposal to build a fifty-thousand-seat stadium in the Meadowlands sports complex. Steinbrenner has rejected proposals to keep the Yankees in the Bronx. . . . The war [to attract or keep businesses] is bad news for taxpayers. The Regional Plan Association estimates that incentive packages given away in the past continue to cost New York, New Jersey, and Connecticut one billion dollars in lost tax revenue annually. 'If we had invested that money in our roads and subways and airports instead of giving it away piecemeal, all of the states would be more competitive and have larger tax bases,' said Claude Shostal, the association president."

—*A* New York Daily News *story lays out the grim facts.*

"The only good thing about having power is that you can use it to help other people."
—The Boss's personal philosophy on life at the top.

Help people. Uh huh.

Bargaining maneuver? Bluster? Frank psychotic episode? Sometimes it was hard to tell *what* was going on when Steinbrenner started talking about vacating the world's most famous ballyard. In the end, the answer to the question "Where will the Yankees play in the twenty-first century?" seems to depend on which group of taxpayers the Boss believes he can most thoroughly shake down.

Whether or not the Bronx Bombers commit the final sacrilege and evacuate the hallowed confines of Yankee Stadium, Steinbrenner deserves to be keelhauled for the way he's forced cash-strapped local governments to stumble over themselves in pursuit of the Yankees. The matter is—or ought to be—simple: The Yankees should play at Yankee Stadium, and because they are one of baseball's fat-cable-contract, big-market teams, taxpayers shouldn't be squeezed dry in order to make that happen. Even *Red Sox* fans got a little choked up about the prospect of abandoning the New York site of the most enduring rivalry in all of baseball. When *they* start agreeing with dyed-in-the-wool Yankee people, you know something's off somewhere. (By the way, some people are talking about tearing down Fenway Park, too. Hey, when you stop to think about it, does the President really have to live at the White House? Wouldn't it be easier to arrange security at a condominium somewhere?)

Tradition? Who needs it? Who needs plaques and memories and nostalgia and continuity? Who needs memories of Babe Ruth and Joe DiMaggio and Phil Rizzuto and Yogi Berra and Mickey Mantle playing *right here*, in a one-of-a-kind stadium and shrine that many consider to be the heart of the American baseball experience, renovated though it may be? Who, for that matter, needs memories of the Yankee Stadium exploits of the Steinbrenner championship teams of 1977, 1978, and 1996? Who needs the sense of ritual associated with actually going *to the place* where all these players built up the greatest dynasty in major-league baseball? Who needs the hassle?

Not George, apparently. Sadly, Steinbrenner's opportunistic grumblings have not yet resulted in legislation prohibiting teams like the Yankees from being able to call themselves the Yankees if they decide to move away from the municipalities that have supported them under that name for the better part of a #$%$@! century. The Powers That Be ought to make sure such laws make it onto the books and quick.

I hate Steinbrenner . . . because he keeps threatening to move the Yankees out of Yankee Stadium, and he may just do it.

24. Let Us Attack the Very Sportswriters With Whom We Habitually Strive to Plant Leaks

Steinbrenner made the following remark to *Sixty Minutes* reporter Harry Reasoner: "Every time somebody wants to be critical of the media and the Fourth Estate, I stop and think where we would have been in this country without them. Because they, they're our conscience."

Steinbrenner has a funny way of showing his gratitude to the members of the Fourth Estate who serve as his conscience.

During a 1987 written tirade against Yankee manager Lou Piniella, Steinbrenner leveled this snide dismissal against the representatives of the Fourth Estate: "I don't know of too many people—even sportswriters—who, if their boss told them to be available for a call at a certain time, wouldn't be there." Does this count as being "critical of the media"?

New York Times sportswriter Murray Chass, who ought to know, has pointed out that Steinbrenner's tenure as Yankee boss has been marked by an early tendency to be "furious" with the press when it wrote critically about him, a midperiod exhilaration at seeing his own name spread far and wide, a return to the furious phase, and, eventually, an intriguing combination of both modes that has marked his later years. Through it all, it's fair to say that Steinbrenner himself could conceivably be considered one of those who occasionally opts to be "critical of the media"—even though he delights in simultaneously feeding members of the media stories meant to further personal grudges or otherwise advance his sinister and all-too-often mysterious agenda.

Leaving aside for a moment the significant entertainment value of Steinbrenner's transparent brand of hypocrisy in press relations, George's absurd statement to Harry Reasoner reflects a serious prob-

lem. It is virtually impossible to know when you're getting the truth from this man.

Are we *surprised* that a fair number of journalists—and others—unload on him?

I hate Steinbrenner . . . for his habit of flying off in a rage when he can't make the press bend to his every misguided, inaccurate, or downright misleading whim.

25. Let Us Now Verbally Attack a Representative of the Office of the Commissioner of Baseball

"It fell to Bill [Murray, former controller with the New York Mets] to telephone George to say the deal would not pass muster. . . . He told Murray he had made an enemy for life, warning him to keep looking over his shoulder because he would be after him, no matter how long it took."
   —*Former Commissioner Bowie Kuhn recalls a staff member's memorable encounter with Steinbrenner.*

Kill-the-messenger hour, huh?
   This was George's outburst to a representative of the commissioner's office who had drawn the dream assignment of passing along the news that the Yankees had exceeded predetermined monetary limits. That trade would have sent Jason Thompson to the Yankees for three players and $850,000. Does it make you feel better or

worse about Steinbrenner that he apparently never subjected Kuhn himself to such tirades during one-on-one encounters? Let's answer that question by posing another one. How much can you respect a person who saves all the badgering for people who can't talk back?

Granted, this all took place back when we *had* a commissioner's office. A place where someone who wasn't an owner could tell Steinbrenner no—through an underling, mind you, but it could be done.

I hate Steinbrenner . . . because he often saves his loudest tirades for powerless messengers.

26. Let Us Now Badmouth the Interim Commissioner of Baseball

"Solely from his contract with a local cable company, New York Yankees owner George Steinbrenner receives $50 million a year. Franchises in small markets cannot dream of matching such sums. This is the nub of the trouble that stole the October Classic from American boys and girls. The Steinbrenners of the game do not want to be forced to share their toll receipts from the infotainment highway with colleagues in the sticks. Speaking of his fellow owner in Milwaukee (who happens to be the interim commissioner of major-league baseball), Steinbrenner told the *Globe:* 'I'd rather die than give a nickel to Bud Selig.' "
    —*Steinbrenner makes his feelings crystal clear.*

Does it matter that the man Steinbrenner is dissing in print is, theoretically, at least, in charge of overseeing major-league baseball? Apparently not. Okay. Just checking. Fire away.

Bud Selig is a fellow owner. Do you think he's in a workable (or even vaguely objective) position to take on the Yankee boss for outrageous remarks that leave fans wondering whether *anybody* is at the helm of the ship? Again: The commissioner's office, once upon a time, served as a check upon the excesses of renegade owners. Why do you suppose that office doesn't seem to exist anymore?

I hate Steinbrenner . . . because now that there's no one to threaten him with expulsion, he has no compunction about attacking the nominal head of the major leagues in print.

27. Another Fascinating Option—Verbally Attacking Fellow Owners Who *Aren't* Bud Selig

There follows a flashback to the good old days when the Boss *could* get called on the carpet for something.

Steinbrenner's withering assessment of Chicago White Sox owner Jerry Reinsdorf and his partner Eddie Einhorn ("The Abbott and Costello of baseball") led to trouble. It came after the Yankee organization had signed former Chicago outfielder Steve Kemp to a multiyear contract. The Boss was fined $5,000 for the remark.

A little test to take at home. If you had to think of a contemporary owner who summoned up memories of a comedy team whose routines consisted of unrelenting badgering, running insults, and perpetual incompetence, and whose most famous routine involved having a conniption fit over a baseball team, would the name "Jerry Reinsdorf" or "Eddie Einhorn" *really* be the first ones you'd come up with?

Here's your basic no-brainer: Owners taking shots at each other in public is bad for the game. (But it's not *as* bad as taking shots at the interim commissioner or the representatives of the commissioner's office.)

I hate Steinbrenner . . . because he shoots his mouth off at other owners without considering the long-term effects on the game of baseball as a whole.

28. Still Another Fascinating Option—Plunging Into Schoolyard Mode and Implying That Physical Violence Is the Best Way to Deal With Representatives of Rival Big-League Operations

"Fort Apache, Yankee Stadium."
　　—Mets executive Frank Cashen's assessment of the Yankee's home field.

"If Frank Cashen made that comment, it doesn't surprise me, because I've never thought much of Frank Cashen. I don't want a remark by a man I have so little respect for to upset my fine relationship with [New York Mets owners] Nelson Doubleday and

Fred Wilpon, but if Mr. Cashen cares to come and discuss the comment with me in a room somewhere . . ."

—*Steinbrenner's response to the press when asked about Cashen's remarks.*

Cashen was apparently under the impression his comment was off the record. All the same, it was a pretty good line. Even if he *had* been trying to crack a joke for public consumption, what's with the "I'll-get-you-after-class" routine? Give the Boss a raspberry for missing the gag.

By the way, what would have happened if Cashen had shown up in a room somewhere? Maybe the Boss would have dropped him like a bag of peat moss. Maybe the Boss is a lean, mean, fighting machine.

We'll never know.

I hate Steinbrenner . . . because he does the world's least convincing Bad, Bad Leroy Brown imitation.

29. Okay, Maybe He's *Not* a Charter Member of the Rick Cerone Fan Club

"Your strikeout to end the game with a man on third carries little weight with me. Stupid mental errors like rounding first too far does. Your vulgarities to me in the clubhouse afterward is water off a duck's back. It was said out of frustration, just as my

45

answer back to you was said out of anger. It has no bearing at all, and I want you to know that."

—*Steinbrenner's note to Rick Cerone after the catcher responded to the Yankee owner's 1981 lectures about "stupid, stupid baserunning" in a playoff game.*

So. Are you the least bit curious about the remark from Cerone that inspired this fascinating combination of ham-handed authoritarianism and pathetically off-center social skills? Sure you are.

Cerone, whose misstep at first base inspired the "stupid, stupid, baserunning" remark, apparently had had one too many of the Boss's locker-room pep talks. The catcher reportedly spoke his mind to the Boat Man as follows: "F— you, George!"

How about *that?* No two ways about it, Cerone's response was a daring, high-degree-of-difficulty rejoinder, a real take-this-job-and-shove-it maneuver. The comeback earned the catcher the respect of players and fans alike for years to come.

Steinbrenner, without missing a beat, then botched his *written* apology following Cerone's (thoroughly understandable) outburst. He turned the note into yet another harangue—a written one, this time. Does the man know how to defuse a tense situation, or what?

For those of you following along at home, here's the rough translation to English from Boss-speak:

"Hey, I know things got out of hand a while back, and I just wanted to drop you a note and let you know I'm ready to bury the hatchet.

That mistake you made, that stupid, stupid mistake I got all worked up about? I just want you to know that that whole issue—as far as I'm concerned, ah—I don't think that particular mistake was so. . . . Actually, it still *really* bugs me, now that I come to think about it. It was just a stupid, stupid mistake and right now it makes me feel like pouring a bagful of rotten kumquats on your head. But there *were* some idiotic things you did that I *am* willing to overlook. Like that *other* mistake you made, the one that was almost as stupid as the really stupid, stupid one that still makes me absolutely furious. That *other* one I'm willing to drop, practically without discussing, no rotten kumquats or anything. So there we go. People get tense sometimes. Harsh words come out, nobody really means them. No hard feelings. I want you to know that."

It could have been worse. Steinbrenner could have chastised Cerone for his stupid, stupid habit of wearing his hat backward while playing defense.

Clearly, we're dealing with an ego of such surrealistically swollen and misshapen proportions that no amount of documentation can possibly do it justice. Can't hurt to try, though. Let's keep going.

I hate Steinbrenner . . . for hounding Rick Cerone and for failing to disengage from countless pointless, ego-driven disputes when virtually anyone else on the face of the earth would have done so.

30. Wake-up Call

"Six in the morning California time, [Steinbrenner] called Bob Erra, and said, more or less, 'Erra! What's going on here? We don't have a twenty-three-million-dollar deal!'

"Still in bed, Bob said, 'You're in the shipbuilding business. When you give your employees a cost-of-living increase, doesn't it compound?' No comment. . . . George hung up, fuming. He knew he'd screwed up."

> —*George shows off those world-famous business and negotiating skills for Bob Erra, a member of Dave Winfield's inner circle. The slugger's contract was eventually renegotiated in such a way that allowed cost-of-living payments to be computed somewhat less aggressively.*

So he's not always a whiz with numbers. A million here, a million there. Hey. You could lose track, too.

Notice the Boss's tactless obliviousness to time differences between the east and west coasts. File the whole thing under "getting the relationship off on the wrong foot." By the way, if *Winfield's* side had misestimated something, how do you think the Boss would have responded to a request to change the deal?

I hate Steinbrenner . . . for those stupid, stupid, mathematical errors—and for giving Winfield endless grief about a legitimately negotiated contract later on down the line.

31. How to Get Way Too Worked Up About Spring Training Games

"I'm paying him $100,000 a year and he can't catch the ball."
  —*Steinbrenner's reaction to a Bobby Murcer error during a spring training contest.*

"Do you want to be fired right now?"
  —*Steinbrenner to manager Billy Martin, in the clubhouse and in front of Martin's players, during spring training, 1977. Steinbrenner was exercising his right to dress down Yankee players himself, a right that would be exercised again and again during the Boss's reign. This was one of the earliest conflicts in the complicated, ongoing feud the owner and the manager would pursue over the years.*

There's a reason they call them exhibition games: They don't really count toward the regular-season standings. Enjoy the sun. Have a margarita. Relax and work on your tan. If it could work for Bob Dole, it could work for you.

Typically, managers use spring training games as an opportunity to let players loosen up and reacquaint themselves with the long-established routines of the game in a (relatively) low-pressure environment. Sure, there are important decisions to be made about rosters and starting jobs, but when it comes to established veterans and current managers, most experienced baseball people realize that the name of the game is basically Back Off Until Opening Day.

Apparently, this is not the George Steinbrenner way. Nothing can be fun. Nothing can be leisurely. Nothing can be done for the simple joy of established, unhurried, anything-could-happen ritual. It's all brain surgery.

He has encouraged turmoil and dissension at Yankee spring training sessions by ripping players for their performance during meaningless games (see previous page), ripping promising young prospects for their performance during meaningless games, and even ripping *umpires* for their performance during meaningless games. Has anyone got a chill pill to pass along?

Do you ever find yourself wondering how the guy would handle, say, coaching a Little League squad? Some encounters are best left to the imagination.

I hate Steinbrenner . . . for his overaggressive, thoroughly inappropriate outbursts during spring training sessions which only serve to increase overall fan cynicism during what ought to be one of the most enjoyable rituals in all of sport.

32. Thanks for a Great Year, Guys

We've seen how George can take the preseason too seriously. Should it come as any surprise that he'd register a zero on the class meter in the aftermath of a World Series defeat?

After his club fell to the Los Angeles Dodgers in 1981, Steinbrenner issued a public apology "for the performance of the Yankees in the World Series." This display of Bossian pique, which inaugurated a fourteen-year Yankee absence from postseason play, was a taste of the bad things to come.

Let's grant, for the sake of argument, that not every owner would have shaken off a World Series loss with perfect grace. Let's further grant that some owners are, like George, always on the lookout for interesting ways to generate press about the hometown club. Even an owner who was a poor loser, even a supremely attention-hungry owner *might* decide to avoid further ill will among the fans—and let a strike-marred season pass without supplying additional evidence that his pathological need for headlines extended even to trashing his own team. Such an owner *might* decide to cool it, just for a change of pace. In this case, he didn't.

Not surprisingly, team morale and on-field performance both went into the tank the following season. And that's not all. Awful, awful things happened to the Yankees with mind-numbing regularity for about ten straight years after the Boss launched this, his most self-serving piece of media manipulation to date. It doesn't take a rocket scientist to see some correlation.

I hate Steinbrenner . . . for using the media to show up his own pennant-winning ballclub.

33. That Legendary Ability to Take a Joke

"The more we lose, the more he'll fly in. And the more he flies in, the better chance that there'll be a plane crash."
—*Graig Nettles, circa 1978.*

Steinbrenner nursed a major grudge against Nettles for his habit of coming up with quotable one-liners like this—and for daring to publish his wry observations on life with the Yankees in book form. The two parted on bad terms (as so many good players have after getting on the Boss's bad side). Suffice it to say that if you're looking for an audience with which to try out new material, or considering a wacky new practical joke, Steinbrenner may not be your best man to pick out in a crowd.

Nettles was a very funny ballplayer. He just made jokes about the wrong topics. So he was sent into exile—whence he helped San Diego win the pennant.

Real leaders know how to let jokes—and, yes, even attacks disguised as jokes—roll off them like water off a duck's back. They don't use them as excuses to begin and escalate feuds . . . and then wonder why members of the team turn against them.

I hate Steinbrenner . . . for letting his own pathetically underdeveloped sense of humor propel him into personnel decisions that were not in the best long-term interests of the New York Yankees.

34. Ring, Ring—Is This the Dugout?

"One call . . . came to the dugout in the middle of a game. [Third baseman Graig] Nettles answered. 'It's George,' he called to [manager Billy] Martin.

" 'You gotta be kidding,' " Billy said.

" 'No,' Nettles said. 'It's really George.'

"Martin still didn't believe Nettles. The manager grabbed the phone. 'Who is this?' he demanded.

" 'George,' said the caller.

" 'Don't be calling me during the game, you asshole,' Martin snapped and slammed the receiver down."

—*An early example of a classic Steinbrenner reach-out-and-touch-some-one technique. Supposedly, when Martin hung up the phone, he was still under the impression he'd been talking to an impostor. Apparently he hadn't.*

Thank God this man does not own the Mayo Clinic. He'd probably call "his" surgeons from Florida during emergency procedures in order to offer suggestions on how to proceed with "his" patients? Why not? It's "his" operating room, right? But remember: If anyone dies on the table during a call, that's because the physician in question is incompetent.

No one but the managers who have worked for him can honestly say how much aggravation this patented Steinbrenner amateur-hour maneuver has caused since its first appearance. The rest of us can take a guess though.

I hate Steinbrenner ... for his record of frequent, uninformed calls to the dugout.

35. Ring, Ring—Is This the Training Room?

"One day we're in the training room being worked on and there's a phone call in trainer Gene Monahan's office. Gene says quietly, head down, 'It's for you, Rickey. It's George.' Rickey [Henderson] gets off the training table, goes into the back room, shuts the door behind him and gets on the horn. After a short while, he emerges, totally bewildered. 'He's crazy. He doesn't believe I'm hurt. He's saying he's going to dock my pay if I don't play. . . .'"
    —*Dave Winfield recalls the most terrifying words in all of Yankeedom:*
      "It's for you. It's George."

Here we have yet another situation a different owner might, *just might,* have left to the field manager. Not the Boss though. Harassing managers over the dugout phone during games wasn't enough. He moved on to the players in the training room. What's next? Between-inning calls to the john to upbraid field personnel who have some-how deviated from the Boss's tough standards?

If you call in sick at George's shipbuilding company, do you suppose he hops in the car and heads over to your apartment and tells you to stick out your tongue and say "ah"? Would you bet against the possibility? Me neither.

I hate Steinbrenner . . . for all manner of innovative, unwelcome meddling with people who ought to be allowed to focus on major-league baseball (rather than George).

36. What Was That They Were Chanting?

"You think this is funny? You think this is a goddamned joke? Didn't you hear what they were saying? 'Steinbrenner sucks!' 'Steinbrenner sucks!' You think that's funny?"
  —*Steinbrenner's rant to coach Jeff Torborg after the legendary game of April 27, 1982, in which Yankee fans made their true feelings about King George known.*

The cause of the now-famous chant from the stands: a home run to right field by Reggie Jackson, whom Steinbrenner had ripped in the press and allowed to depart New York at the conclusion of the previous season. As a result, the much-maligned slugger was now playing for the California Angels. The Boss called an emergency meeting after the game to discuss the dire situation in depth; Torborg had some (understandable) difficulty keeping a straight face through the proceedings.

In 1990 Yankee stadium fans served up a rousing standing ovation when George was banished from baseball for the second time. (Like the rest of us they probably thought that one would stick.) One wonders what the emergency meeting of the Yankee inner circle sounded like on that occasion, if any such meeting was called. One hopes no one in the room snickered at an inopportune moment.

Survival tactic: *Don't crack up* when the Boss is trying to figure what the Esteemed Master of San Clemente would do if faced with a similar situation during the Watergate crisis.

I hate Steinbrenner . . . for his tactic of engaging in pointless, self-serving tirades while in the company of seasoned baseball professionals who shouldn't have to listen to his lawn fertilizer.

37. And the Worst Choice of Words Award Goes To . . .

"One day in Fort Lauderdale, [Steinbrenner] came up to Al [Frohman] and said, 'You better tell your boy to start hitting.' Al replied, 'He's not a boy. Go f____ yourself.' End of conversation."

   —*Dave Winfield reminisces about Steinbrenner's demonstration of his way of winning points with new members of the Yankee family.*

In one concise sentence we may have come across the quintessential George utterance: "You better tell your boy to start hitting." Here we have, in a bare eight words, proof of the Boss's jaw-dropping insensitivity to the connotation of certain common terms as they relate to members of racial minorities; the Boss's working assumption that he more or less owns the people who work for him; his willingness to ruin the leisurely atmosphere of spring training games with his endless badgering of innocent people; his ability to put star players on the spot; and, in the Boss's overemphasis on hitting performance during games that *don't count*, a general ignorance about baseball.

If only Frohman (a member of Winfield's inner circle) had been a manager instead! George could have attempted to fire him for talking back, made a whole bunch of headlines, and then paid somebody a huge amount of money to gather nasty information about him. Then we'd have pretty much covered all the bases.

George is not a racist. He's a nincompoop.

For the record, the much browbeaten Winfield drove in 100 runs a year for five straight seasons with the Yankees. Can you imagine what might have been if he hadn't had to deal with garbage like this?

I hate Steinbrenner . . . for his consistent failure to understand that poorly chosen words poison relationships and make it harder to win baseball games.

38. "Mr. May" Turns Into Mr. World Series Hero

"After becoming the oldest [player] to homer in a Series . . . 41-year-old Dave Winfield garnered the series-winning hit."
 —*Winfield puts on a display in 1992 for the Toronto Blue Jays that erases the Boss's derogatory "Mr. May" label once and for all.*

A few years earlier Steinbrenner had ripped Dave Winfield, labeling the outfielder "Mr. May" for his supposed inability to come through in clutch late-season situations. By doing so, of course, the Boss subtly reminded us all about how much he'd appreciated Reggie Jackson, Mr. October, during *his* tenure as a player at Yankee Stadium.

Did Winfield have a great World Series in 1981? No. Did he deserve to have his reputation besmirched in the New York media by the Last Messenger of Congeniality? No again. The real problem behind the Yankees' long (1981–1990) winter of discontent, under-achievement, and morale meltdown lies with the man at the head of the organization, not the top-notch outfielder he so habitually maligned.

The "Mr. May" remark was only the most memorable gibe of the many that marked Steinbrenner's ongoing public fixation on the shortcomings of his star player. For his pointless, seemingly endless public thrashing of a superb player he himself had courted assiduously, the Boss deserves a big, fat boo from the bleachers.

I hate Steinbrenner . . . because he had the nerve to appeal to the mystique of Mr. October—Reggie Jackson—when it was the Boss himself who had permitted number 44 to move on to new pastures.

39. You, Too, Can Attack the Competence and Integrity of Major-League Umpires—But You May Not Make Front-Page News

"[He's] not a capable umpire. He doesn't measure up."
  —*Steinbrenner's public assessment of an American League umpire (who shall go mercifully nameless here).*

The public remark brought about legal squabbles with the Umpires Association. In 1987 Steinbrenner's right to launch media assaults on umpires who had fallen from his favor was upheld by a New York state appeals court.

Steinbrenner blasts everybody. Why should umpires be any different? This tiff with the Umpires Association wasn't the Boss's only needless conflict with the game's on-field arbiters. Steinbrenner once claimed that an umpire had been instructed to rule in the favor of the National League on close plays—during *spring training*. Rumor has it that Steinbrenner has even encouraged Yankee Stadium personnel to show disputed plays on the DiamondVision scoreboard. Who can say whether he's engaged in such idiocy? Sure, it's *interesting,* but talk about making life more difficult than it has to be for the men who make the calls . . .

George keeps an eye out for when people screw up in a high-profile way and then makes the most of it in the media or whatever other incredibly visible public forum he can track down. If quality control consisted only of the act of howling about other people's mistakes and making others feel small, George would have led the revolution. Unfortunately, nattering on about details others have missed *doesn't* always lead to improved performance.

I hate Steinbrenner ... because irresponsible public remarks from an owner leveled at big-league umpires reinforce overall fan cynicism about the game—cynicism that is already at dangerously high levels, thank you very much.

40. The Eerie Nixon Connections

"Attempting to influence employees to behave dishonestly is the kind of misconduct which, if ignored by baseball, would undermine the public's confidence in our game. . . . I have decided to place Mr. Steinbrenner on the ineligible list for a period of two years. In accordance, he is declared ineligible and incompetent to manage or advise in the management of the affairs of the New York Yankees."
   —*Bowie Kuhn's November 27, 1974 statement suspending Steinbrenner*

"I am not a crook."
> —*The guiding message behind Richard Nixon's damage-control campaign of the year before . . . a mantra that certain of the president's supporters may have appropriated for their own private use when the going got tough in the mid-seventies. Its effectiveness in all situations, however, is open to question.*

Nowadays, Steinbrenner's illegal campaign contributions to Tricky Dick's reelection effort are only the first in a long, disquieting series of Nixonian self-destruction/self-revival efforts. The guiding principle: The bigger the fall, the grander the comeback—so read the teachings of the Master of San Clemente.

We have to ask ourselves then: *Is Steinbrenner baseball's Nixon?* This is kind of like the list of unsettling Lincoln/Kennedy connections. Stick with me, okay?

Nixon was counted out by the experts in 1952, 1956, and 1962 but eventually slouched toward Bethlehem, as it were, to be reborn in 1968, when he finally won the White House. There he oversaw a time-released national trauma of an administration that terminated in obstruction of justice and Nixon's own resignation in disgrace. Steinbrenner was suspended but eventually found his way back into major-league baseball. He too would screw up in bigger and more agonizing ways.

Nixon appears to have tried to fire everyone and everything in sight during the celebrated Saturday Night Massacre in 1973. The campaign-funds fracas inspired manager Billy Martin's celebrated 1978 remark about Reggie Jackson and Steinbrenner: "One's a born

liar, and the other's convicted." That zinger cost Billy his job—for a while, that is, until Steinbrenner could rehire him and then fire him again for something else. It was the first shot in what might be called a state of Perpetual Saturday Night Massacre that settled over the Bronx for the next decade or so.

As it happened, Nixon inched his way toward his final comeback goal—respectability—after being pardoned by Gerald Ford. As it happened, Steinbrenner served only fifteen months of the two-year suspension Kuhn imposed for the illegal campaign contributions and was pardoned by Ronald Reagan.

Gives you the chills, doesn't it?

Steinbrenner *might* be baseball's Nixon—but do baseball fans really deserve that particular nightmare? By the by, the assault on the U.S. Constitution perpetrated by the Nixon administration has intriguing parallels in Steinbrenner's views on free speech in public places (as we'll see a little bit later).

Truth-in-advertising note: A writer who's assembling a collection of the Boss's foul-ups might be tempted, throughout that book, to harp sarcastically, and at even the slightest provocation, on the many disconcerting similarities between the departed Master of San Clemente and the principal owner of the New York Yankees.

But it would be wrong. That's for sure.

I hate Steinbrenner . . . because he represents a walking Long National Nightmare for the game of baseball—a nightmare that steadfastly refuses to end.

41. The Eerie Roy Cohn Connections

"George's counsel, Roy Cohn, was arguably the sleaziest lawyer in the country."

—A shrewd assessment from Dave Winfield of the man for whom ruthless lawyer jokes might as well have been invented.

George Steinbrenner and Roy Cohn. Could you make this stuff up? Do you even want to imagine what a conversation between George Steinbrenner and Roy Cohn might have *sounded* like?

For those unfamiliar with Cohn's exploits, some background information is probably in order. There aren't too many people who knew Cohn, or knew of him, who would quibble with Winfield's characterization of the notorious, mercilessly ambitious lawyer, a protégé of none other than J. Edgar Hoover *and* Joe McCarthy. The nastiness-personified attorney was the subject of not one but *two* revealing, disturbing character studies in recent years: a memorable biopic starring James Woods *(Citizen Cohn)* and an extraordinary play by Tony Kushner *(Angels in America)*. Cohn, a well-connected but ethically myopic wheeler-dealer, pretty much destroyed, or attempted to destroy, nearly everyone in his path over the course of his sadly unforgettable legal career. He wrote a book entitled *How to Stand Up for Your Rights and Win*. He could have written one entitled *How to Lose Friends, Infuriate People, and Generate Bad Karma*. Why Steinbrenner would want to conduct business with him in any way, shape, or form remains a mystery even to the Boss's many adversaries.

How messed up was this dude? Cohn made even the Boss look good by comparison. Maybe we should give thanks that Steinbrenner didn't make him General Manager.

I hate Steinbrenner . . . for choosing one of the single most despicable figures of the latter part of the twentieth century to help illustrate the maxim, "You're best known by the company you keep."

42. Look at Me, I'm in the Dictionary

The 1995 *Cambridge Dictionary of American Biography* lists Steinbrenner among its "Americans from all walks of life who have contributed in the past and who contribute now to all the disciplines covered." The Boss's entry, however, focuses quite briefly on his "contributions" to the game of baseball and soberly notes that Steinbrenner's "pursuit of free agency" led to on-field success. It points out, too, that "he was constantly involved in controversies with players and managers, usually ending in their abrupt departure." The Steinbrenner entry also reviews the Howie Spira debacle that led to George's departure from the game in 1990, as well as his 1993 return to the game.

Put it all together, and there's still more evidence, as though we needed it, that *bad* press can win you the attention you're after—and, by any reasonable standard, far more attention than you deserve. Consider, if you will, that the article on Steinbrenner's "contributions" to the national pastime runs longer than the articles profiling such luminaries of the game as Dizzy Dean, Sandy Koufax, Jimmie Foxx,

Cool Papa Bell, and Happy Chandler—the man who okayed Jackie Robinson's entry to the major leagues.

Can you say "perspective check"?

I hate Steinbrenner . . . because his shenanigans have allowed him to overshadow some of the game's true giants.

43. How I Won the World Series . . . Very Quietly

The selection criteria in the abovementioned *Dictionary of American Biography* may just be subject to debate—and so, alas, may its ability to double-check the work of its researchers. Steinbrenner's entry in the reference work credits the Boss's efforts for the New York Yankees' world championship season of 1979.

There's only one problem. The Pittsburgh Pirates, not the New York Yankees, won the Fall Classic that year. The Yankees finished fourth, behind the Eastern Division, and eventually American League, champion Baltimore Orioles.

I hate Steinbrenner . . . because, even though he's gotten credit in a highly respected reference resource for a World Series championship that his organization never won, he remains fitfully surly about his press coverage. If missing the playoffs by 13½ games, and then going into the books as the brains behind a world championship outfit doesn't count as catching a break from the media, then I don't know what does.

67

44. Let Me Make One Thing Perfectly Clear

"I used to be very hands-on, but lately I've been more hands-off, and I plan to become more hands-on and less hands-off and hope that hands-on will become better than hands-off, the way hands-on used to be."
   —*Steinbrenner in 1990 on his philosophy of ownership.*

During the very darkest days of the Watergate crisis, George's hero Richard Nixon also rambled a little bit. Unfortunately Henry Kissinger wasn't kneeling next to the Boss to lend moral support at the time Steinbrenner made these remarks, so they're probably even more cryptic than they would otherwise have been.

   Actually the Boss has a completely valid point here. It's just that his remarks could probably benefit from a little expert clarification from a seasoned Steinbrenner watcher (like yours truly). What he shared with us on this occasion was just a bit too subtle for the average baseball fan to understand without help. So here goes.

   The thing people don't understand about hands-off as opposed to hands-on is that hands-off isn't necessarily *exclusive* of hands-on. Hands-off can actually serve as a kind of necessary supplement to hands-on, even though hands-off doesn't—and can't—take place at the same time as hands-on. If you've got hands-off, you need hands-on, but not *at the same time* as hands-on, because even though hands-off exists in the same fundamental way hands-on exists, no amount of hands-off can bring hands-on into focus while hands-off is in effect. Without an appreciation of *both* hands-off and hands-on, even hands-off *or* hands-on loses hands down. Got it?

I hate Steinbrenner . . . because he sometimes shows as little concern for the use of the English language as he shows for the long-term interests of the game of baseball.

45. A Monkey Trying to Do What?

"What the hell were you doing out there? Jesus! You looked like a monkey trying to screw a football out there."
    —*Steinbrenner's comment to an infielder who had made a fielding error.*

Doesn't this remark sound like someone's deep, half-remembered Freudian dream, one you'd rather not have to analyze? Let's not analyze it, then.

Does anybody know whether any children were within hearing range of this particular zinger? Other than Steinbrenner, that is? In keeping with major-league baseball's ongoing attempt to reinforce its ties to the American family, and with due respect for the high bowdlerization standard set by the Great Man of San Clemente upon the release of his White House conversations in transcript form, it seems appropriate to edit, judiciously, the above sharp-tongued remark. The passage above *should* have read:

"What the [location of eternal damnation deleted] were you doing out there? [Divine characterization deleted]! You looked like you were a [primate characterization deleted] trying to [sexually oriented verb deleted] a [sporting-equipment product reference deleted] out there!"

Please accept the author's and publisher's apologies for the failure to substitute this version of Steinbrenner's insult for the unexpurgated one. It won't happen again. Unless something manages to slip past.

I hate Steinbrenner . . . for talking about *football* when he gets really worked up. He can't even *swear* like a real baseball guy.

46. How Shall I Put This . . .

THE BOSS WATCH

"Your husband f___ed up the game for us!"
  —*Steinbrenner to the wife of Yankee third-base coach Ron Ferraro. Ferraro had given Willie Randolph the green light, allowing Randolph to try to score from first on a double during a playoff game against the Kansas City Royals in 1980. Randolph was thrown out. According to the July 4, 1995,* New York Times, *Steinbrenner later had Ferraro fired.*

Subtle, huh? What do you think he'd have said if he'd been sitting next to Ferraro's mom?

Let's face it. The man loses his cool at any and every opportunity. Given half a chance, he'd chew out Mother Teresa.

I hate Steinbrenner . . . for using decidedly ungentlemanly language in assessing Ron Ferraro's performance with Ferraro's wife—and for subjecting countless other innocent bystanders who have no professional connection to his unique brand of invective.

47. My Boss's Name? I'd Rather Not Say.

The focus of this entry—folks who worked for or reported to George who had nothing whatsoever to do with the New York Yankees. (He's a business tycoon in all sorts of areas, you know.) What's it like to work for George outside the pressure cooker that is big-league baseball? Let's find out.

"There was no excuse for those ice chunks in the ice cream. I demanded to know who was in charge of the food quality."
  —*The Boss explaining a sudden 1981 eruption, one that sounds like it must have alarmed diners in the restaurant of the Bay Harbor Inn—owned by Steinbrenner.*

"Company headquarters [of the American Ship Building Company], once staffed with about 30 employees, is down to 11, many of whom tremble at the mention of the Boss's name."
—*Less than exemplary levels of morale at George's "other" operation.*

"Once [Steinbrenner] had the switchboard operator in a Boston hotel fired because she wouldn't allow him to place a long distance call from the telephone in a bar, as per regulation."
—*It's so hard to get good help these days. People simply insist on following the rules.*

You were expecting maybe that he was *nice* to everyone who worked for him or had to report to him outside of the Yankee organization?

Being nasty to people who have no way to establish or maintain appropriate limits is pretty much the entire Steinbrenner Paradox—a paradox that applies to any number of self-centered, money-hungry black holes masquerading as leaders in this diverse society of ours.

The paradox is this: Usually, when people like George Steinbrenner abuse you verbally, you can't talk back. At the same time you can't keep your mouth shut and maintain any self-respect. You have no option other than quitting, which is, in its way, a sick kind of victory for the pseudoleader. You're gone. He's still around.

I hate Steinbrenner . . . for his record of badgering assorted nonbaseball underlings over the years.

48. Alert the Authorities!

George Steinbrenner was in Florida on August 24, 1987, watching the Yankees play the California Angels at Anaheim Stadium on TV. The broadcast appeared to pick up evidence that California pitcher Don Sutton was doing some creative—and illegal—things to the ball.

The Boss called Yankee manager Lou Piniella on the dugout phone and demanded that Piniella protest Sutton's skullduggery. George seems to have overlooked the unfortunate fact that the Yankee pitcher that evening was Tommy John, a hurler who'd been known to manhandle a few baseballs in his time as well. So it was that Piniella explained patiently to his boss that the Yankees were leading, 1–0, and that John was probably just as guilty of doctoring the ball as Sutton. The manager also alerted Steinbrenner to something many Yankee fans no doubt already knew: If the Yankees protested about Sutton, the Angels would respond by making a stink about John . . . an outcome that didn't seem worth pursuing too doggedly while the Yankees were ahead.

The dugout call finally ended. The Yankees won the game, 3–2.

You can say what you want. I think the Boss just wanted to see whether or not *Piniella* knew it was a dumb idea to encourage the Angels to check what Tommy John was throwing.

I hate Steinbrenner . . . for his amply demonstrated ignorance of basic baseball strategy—which wouldn't really be too much of a problem if he didn't have a history of attempting to micromanage his teams.

49. Lou's Brainstorm

"Oh, no you don't . . . you're not going to trick me that easy. I figured out what you're up to. You're the manager. You do the managing. I'm the owner. I'll do the second-guessing."

—*Steinbrenner's response to manager Lou Piniella's ingenious suggestion that the Boss make all the decisions during a spring training game and relay his own managerial moves by issuing signals from the stands.*

At least Richard Nixon actually served in the #$@#! Pacific before he started issuing orders as commander in chief. Whereas George, when offered the opportunity to actually *participate* in the arena about which he claims to know so much . . . Let's just say we all expected more from a man who so obviously admired the Great Man who served with distinction—and suffered so egregiously—as our thirty-seventh president.

Wouldn't you have paid top dollar to see this Steinbrenner-managed game from beginning to end? Wouldn't you have loved to film it for posterity?

I hate Steinbrenner . . . for failing to put his money (as it were) where his mouth is.

50. No, Really, Boss—You Wear It Well

". . . So red he seemed to be wearing lipstick." That's how crimson the Boss's lips looked in a photograph in the 1981 Yankee yearbook due to a printing slipup. After the first few games of the season, Steinbrenner ordered that the unsold copies be removed from their stands.

Isn't there at least a *chance* of divine intervention at the printing press here? Couldn't the Supreme Being have pulled this little trick as a not-so-subtle message to a certain person in the Yankee hierarchy who needed comeuppance on the general inappropriateness of humiliation in public forums? Do you think the Universal Clue Police could have acted any more unmistakably?

I don't know about you, but when random forces conspire to allow the Powers That Be to send important messages *my* way, I don't try to tear up the telegram. Typical overreaction, too. If he just corrects the problem in the next printing, this story is good for a couple of snickers around the ballpark. But seizing literature Not in Accordance With the Party Line Established by Fearless Leader makes sure the whole thing winds up making Steinbrenner look ever so slightly like some contemporary tinhorn tyrant. Let us not forget, by the way, that Jay Leno once referred to Saddam Hussein as "the Steinbrenner of Iraq." It was probably one of Leno's best lines—but in light of incidents like this, it seems less like a gag and more like a documentary.

I hate Steinbrenner . . . because considering all that has happened since 1981, he's clearly incapable of learning basic lessons about how little fun it is to be made to look like an idiot in public.

51. Dubious Declarations of Principle

"I am dead set against free agency. It can ruin baseball."
  —*Steinbrenner to the press during an early point of his tenure as Yankee boss.*

This from the owner who kept pounding the "launch" button on the salary-explosion mechanism in the late seventies. This from the owner who got addicted to headline juice and went looking for new ways to throw huge sacks of money in some of the most unlikely laps in baseball.

Concession to the demands of objectivity: The Boss's dramatic decision to ignore his own airtight, loophole-free pronouncement about free agency helped bring two world championships for the New York Yankees in the late 1970s and one in 1996—the latter providing big-league baseball with a dramatic, come-from-behind Fall Classic it desperately needed after the strike of 1994.

We now return you to your regular program. The Boss's dramatic decision to ignore his own airtight, loophole-free pronouncement about free agency led to the following players donning Yankee pinstripes: Don Gullett, Andy Messersmith, Rudy May, Rick Reuschel, Bob Shirley, John Montefusco, Ed Whitson, Britt Burns, Steve Trout, Tim Leary, and so on. And those are just the *pitchers,* folks. How much, we are entitled to ask, did Danny Tartabull contribute to the cause while he was wearing pinstripes?

What kind of carpenter, as the old saying has it, blames the tools? One man's opinion: Free agency doesn't represent the big threat to baseball. Owners who set world land speed records for contradicting themselves, browbeat everyone with the vaguest connection to Yankee Stadium, and turn their own clubhouses into makeshift psychiatric wards represent the big threat to baseball.

A more detailed discussion of Steinbrenner's Daliesque personnel moves, free-agent-related and otherwise, appears elsewhere in this book. For now let's just remember that the man has a habit of talking earnestly out of both sides of his mouth—and making his listeners wonder, as they did about his hero, whether they'd buy a used car from this man.

Did I mention that he gave lots of money illegally to Richard Nixon's 1972 reelection campaign? I did? Okay. Just checking.

I hate Steinbrenner . . . for first trashing and then relentlessly abusing—as few owners ever have—the free agent process.

52. Less Than Perfect Relations With Those Who Are Curious About His Ball Club's Record as an Employer of Minorities

"I have not been there for two years."

—*Steinbrenner's 1993 response to questions from the press about the Yankees' record as an employer of minorities. The fact that Steinbrenner, recently returned from exile, had been running the Yankees since 1973 (with time off for bad behavior) apparently didn't figure into the equation.*

Lousy Media Management, Advanced Level. Senior Honors Course: How to Tick Off Important Reporters Who Ask Perfectly Legitimate Questions. May I introduce our professor for this semester, Doctor Steinbrenner.

Who cares what anyone, even the *New York Times*, wants to know about how you've handled a sensitive issue in the past? Who cares what else anyone has to say about the Yankee organization's record on a matter likely to attract greater-than-average levels of public interest? Don't answer that question.

Don't treat the senior *New York Times* writer with anything resembling professional courtesy. Don't talk about what's happened in the past and how you want to change it for the better. Just use the magic words: "That's enough."

I hate Steinbrenner . . . for his willingness to stonewall on certain issues of general public interest—the minority hiring record in the Yankee organization, for instance.

53. Less Than Perfect Community Relations in the Bronx

"Community leaders are charging that a Yankee vice president's alleged use of the terms 'monkeys' and 'colored' to describe some Bronx youths are symptomatic of the team's lack of interest in cultivating fans and participating in youth programs in the predominantly non-white borough. Yankee vice president Richard Kraft denies making the comments. 'I don't see an effort on the part of the Yankees to reach out to the community,' Rep. Jose Serrano (D-Bronx) said yesterday. 'It's almost as if the Yankees are always reaching out to the suburbs.' Added State Sen. Pedro Espada (D-Bronx), who has requested a meeting with Yankee owner George Steinbrenner: 'It is clear to me that Mr. Steinbrenner and his corporation hold the Bronx in great disdain.'"

—New York Newsday *describes the Boss's community-relations problems.*

What? Just because he's put down the neighborhood by making all kinds of threats about leaving? You think that means he has some problem with the Bronx?

The Boss has no problem with the Bronx—buddy, it's the Bronx that has the problem with the Boss, because folks in the Bronx probably *think* the Boss *thinks* he has some Bronx sob story, when obviously the Boss has no problem hobnobbing in the Bronx, because the Boss got his chops at the School of Hard Knocks, not out in the 'burbs. But the people in the Bronx keep babbling and blabbing and making a hubbub about some overblown Boss/Bronx "problem." Boy, that's probably the whole problem right there.

No surprise here: The Yankee top management is contemptuous of the team's potential fans *as a whole*. Why shouldn't it be contemptuous of those of its potential fans who also happen to be its neighbors?

I hate Steinbrenner . . . because his organization has had a long history of fostering a culture of paranoia, exclusion, and estrangement. (And that's just inside the clubhouse.)

54. The Greatness That Is Me

Here's Steinbrenner's aggressively self-confident question concerning Gabe Paul, his former general manager: "What did he ever win before he worked with me?"

Okay. So here's the proposition. George Steinbrenner clearly played a more important role in the development of the championship squads of 1977 and 1978 than his front-office people did. Please consider this statement closely . . . and recall, if you will, that this is the man who agreed to trade Jay Buhner for Ken Phelps. (Man, was that trade traumatic for yours truly, or what?)

George may simply have been attempting to follow the example of some interesting role models. After all, Joseph Stalin and the Ayatollah Khomeini ordered that recent history be rewritten, too.

Let's set the larger, more complicated issue of unfettered megalomania aside: The Boss's attempts to steal credit from his former subordinates is a sign of a deeply skewed worldview.

The really scary thing is he appears to *believe* things like the Gabe Paul remark when he says them.

I hate Steinbrenner . . . for taking way too much credit for the 1977 and 1978 World Championship teams.

55. The Greatness That Is Me—Except for, You Know, the Years 1982 to 1993

"Since the Yankees won their first pennant in 1921, they have plodded through two eleven-year periods in which they have won no pennants. Before turning the team around in 1976 for a three-year run in the World Series, Steinbrenner was liable for the last three seasons of the first record drought, and he has presided over the current stretch."

—*Murray Chass details the sad truth in the* New York Times, *July 3, 1993. At the conclusion of that year, the gap between pennants became the longest in New York Yankee history.*

The New York Yankees won the the 1996 World Championship. That year marked the team's first appearance in the Fall Classic since the bizarre 1981 strike season, when they came in first in the first half of the season (thereby clinching a spot in the playoffs), came in sixth in the second half, triumphed in the AL playoffs, and then lost the World Championship to the Los Angeles Dodgers in six games.

The fourteen-year gap between Yankee pennants isn't any individual manager's fault. It can't be, because no one skipper has been left standing for long enough to account for even a sizable fraction of the time in question. The natural question arises then: Who *is* responsible for the longest-ever stretch between American League championships at Yankee Stadium?

Any nominees?

The motion is seconded. For what it's worth, George is also under the gun for the Yankees' longest-ever gap between World Championship seasons (1979–1995) and the entire sorry decade of the 1980s (the Yankees' first decade without a World Championship since 1910–1919).

Some might argue that it was Steinbrenner who most dramatically obeyed the oft-repeated command of many frustrated American League fans of the forties and fifties: "Break up the Yankees!" If the 1990 New York Yankees weren't an example of a broken-up ballclub, nothing was.

I hate Steinbrenner . . . for engineering the longest stretch between pennants in New York Yankee club history. (Of course the drought finally concluded in the 1996 World Championship season, an accomplishment for which the Boss deserves all due credit. Time will tell whether or not another decade and a half wait is in store for Yankee fans.)

56. What Do You Think I Am? The Owner?

"During MSG's Yankees/Indians telecast from Cleveland last Sunday, cameras caught a note being lowered on a television cable to the box where George Steinbrenner and Indians boss Eli Jacobs were sitting. The befuddled owners read it and chuckled. Sources said it was a plea from announcer Tony Kubek to do whatever they could to avert a strike."

> —*Sportswriter Steve Zipay makes it clear that fans and current players aren't the only ones Steinbrenner is willing to ignore when it comes to addressing the long-term interests of the game. Former Yankee players can be laughed off as well.*

Why should Steinbrenner have had any interest in listening to the concerns of a Yankee hero from the team's golden age? The owners were starting in on their catastrophic game of chicken with the players' union. Kubek was only interested in, you know, saving the National Pastime.

You can't hold Steinbrenner responsible for the 1994 strike all by himself, because there were other moneyed fools around, wearing both business suits and warmup jackets, making sure that heartfelt appeals to the long-term interests of the game (like Kubek's) got lost in the shuffle. But you *can* assign ownership as a whole a fair share of the blame for the debacle that was 1994. Give the Boss and all the rest of the Lords of the Realm the raspberry for failing to come to terms with the players in time to avert disaster.

If they all managed to screw things up the *last* time everything started to fall apart, who's to say they won't screw things up the *next* time everything starts to fall apart? With folks like Steinbrenner on the scene, you have to wonder whether it's only a matter of time before the National Pastime endures another meltdown.

I hate Steinbrenner . . . for his role in the bullheaded strike of 1994— and for failing to heed the prestrike appeal of Tony Kubek.

57. No, Really, You'll Love Them, They're Just Like Real Big-Leaguers

" 'We believe that the value of these games is clearly less than games with bonafide major-league players,' Marty Brooks, acting head of MSG Network, said yesterday. 'We first expressed our concern to the Yankees over a month ago and, following a preliminary meeting, the Yankees had ignored our request to meet in an effort to resolve this issue. We hope to meet with the Yankees in the near future to resolve this matter.' . . .

" 'We are very disappointed,' said David Sussman, the Yankees' vice president and general counsel. 'From our perspective, the contract is very clear. These games very clearly are on the regular American League schedule.' "

—*Pete Bowles and Steve Zipay report that the Yankee leadership is shocked, shocked to learn that anyone would have a problem with its plan to field big-league wannabes. The pinstriped uniforms alone are worth every penny MSG Network paid. Who cares who's wearing them?*

Yes. He really tried to pull this off. Aren't you glad the strike didn't extend into the regular season?

Players, shmayers. It's the *franchise* people tune in to see, right? Because owning the Yankees means you own *everything* of any consequence, no matter what anyone else has to say about the situation.

For continued cluelessness and his trademark insensitivity to both fans and players—not to mention broadcast outlets no more eager to be swindled than members of the first two groups—George deserves the goat horns. (Perhaps we're all missing the big picture here, and he was really driven by an altruistic desire to bring as many underqualified athletes as possible in touch with the big-league experience as possible before the strike came to an end.)

I hate Steinbrenner . . . for attempting to stiff-arm cable officials into paying full fees for exhibition games featuring replacement players.

58. The Fine Art of Treating New York Yankee Office Staff Far, Far Worse Than George Costanza Gets Treated on *Seinfeld*

"The bedroom of [Reggie Jackson's] suite had two twin beds. Jackson . . . demanded a change to a suite with king-sized double beds. No such thing existed at the Americana. He demanded to see the hotel manager. He was not available at this late hour. He called George Steinbrenner. . . . Steinbrenner got on the phone to his public relations director, Marty Appel, who had made the arrangements.

" 'You're fired,' screamed Steinbrenner."
   —*A touching episode from the Boss's presigning courtship of Reggie Jackson. The story illustrates the classic Steinbrenner management principle: When presented with a challenging situation, find someone to browbeat. In this case, Steinbrenner exploded at the man responsible for booking Jackson into the Americana suite that had recently served as accommodations for President-elect Jimmy Carter.*

"In his Yankee Stadium box . . . [Steinbrenner] was capable of suddenly screaming at the umpires, the players, the manager, his secretary, his organist, his security people—anyone."
   —*Not our George! The reminiscence is from former Commissioner of Baseball Bowie Kuhn.*

According to the *New York Times*, Steinbrenner once fired a secretary for giving him a sandwich he hadn't ordered.

"Look, I'm going to miss a meeting because you screwed up. Just pack your stuff."

>   —*Steinbrenner's own recollection of his firing a secretary (over the phone and from the airport) because she had not made a plane reservation. Some time later, he decided to make amends by paying her son's college expenses, thereby illuminating another classic Steinbrenner management principle: If You Decide to Throw Money at Someone Afterward, You Get to Act Like a Jerk Whenever You Want.*

Steinbrenner also reportedly "humiliated" a secretary in full view of a bunch of reporters because she brought him the wrong tax form.

Writer and former Yankee star Jim Bouton has argued that Steinbrenner's inexcusable behavior toward his own employees is the main reason the Boss deserves to be dismissed from the game of baseball. It's a point of view. While it's hard to put the Boss's long-running tantrum-fest in the same category as his record with regard to payments and damaging information about his own players, it's just as hard to ignore the fact that one brand of pathetically bad people skills has to be related to the other brand of pathetically bad people skills.

Boorish megalomania is as boorish megalomania does. The fact that one throws around huge amounts of cash after the fact—or, for that matter resuscitates the careers of troubled former major-leaguers—or, for that matter, *boasts* about one's altruistic behavior to members of the media in an attempt to repair one's tattered public image—none of this excuses perpetually aggressive, manipulative, immature behavior by the head of a big-league baseball team.

I hate Steinbrenner . . . for making the whole notion of working for the New York Yankees a running joke for the better part of two and a half decades.

59. The Fine Art of Treating Yankee Clubhouse Staff Like Dirt

THE BOSS WATCH

"Here I've got a strength coach [Jeff Mangold] who can't keep my players from getting hurt, and then I've got this asshole [trainer Gene Monahan] who can't get them healthy again."
—*Steinbrenner's inspiring assessment of clubhouse staff.*

It's time to play—Interpret the Telling Steinbrenner Word Choice! And here we go. Contestants, listen closely.

Clue number 1: *"I've got"* a strength coach.

Clue number 2: *"I've got"* a trainer. In fact *"I've got"* one whom "I" denigrate with abusive language, the better, apparently, to solidify "my" claim to ownership.

Clue number 3: *"I've got"* both of these people. And on whom are these gentlemen of "mine" working? On "my" players. Not "the" players, mind you. Not even "our" players. "My" players.

Okay, contestants, take a good, long look at these clues and then hit the buzzer when you spot the person with the unhealthy desire to own and manipulate other human beings. Bzzzzzap! Very good work, Mr. Berra. Congratulations! You're today's big winner; you move on to our bonus round. The next opening in the Yankee organization will arise in approximately thirty seconds. You have the option to accept it or tactfully decline any association with the present regime for the balance of your life.

Nice call, Mr. Berra.

It had been the author's sincere hope not to have to resort to this next step, but extraordinary times call for extraordinary measures—and you never know, he might actually read this. Ready?

"*Amendment Thirteen, ratified July 9, 1868.* Neither slavery nor involuntary servitude, except as a punishment for crime whereof the party shall have been duly convicted, shall exist within the United States, or any place subject to their jurisdiction. Congress shall have power to enforce this article by appropriate legislation."

There. They can't say I didn't try. And it doesn't hurt to reinforce this stuff. Constitutional amendments *have* been known to be repealed, and George *has* been known to contribute to political movements not necessarily in the best long-term interests of the republic.

I hate Steinbrenner . . . because he has a history of treating Yankee clubhouse personnel like garbage.

60. The Fine Art of Using the Media to Threaten One's Own Front-Office Staff

"I'm getting a little fed up with the whole situation of Stick [Gene Michael] and Buck [Showalter] saying things in meetings and then being Mr. Nice Guy to the press about him [Danny Tartabull]. They should stand up and say what they said at the meetings, or there are going to be serious consequences."

—Steinbrenner to the press before an unhappy—and vocal—Danny Tartabull was finally traded to Oakland in 1995.

Looks like Steinbrenner missed Negotiating 101. Michael and Showalter were trying to trade Tartabull. If they'd talked openly to the press about their misgivings concerning him, they'd have made it that much more difficult for the Yankees to make a good deal.

But why should we hold George responsible for adherence to such fine points? He's only been running this club, in his own inimitable, oblivious way, for about a *quarter of a century,* friends.

Strategy, shmategy. It's George against the enemy, and there are going to be serious consequences if people don't start badmouthing the enemy, dammit. Don't go around trying to get the most you can for an unhappy player. Speak your mind, like you did in the meeting. Tell everyone in baseball this guy's a dud and out to make everyone's life miserable. Drive his price down, and I mean now. Go out there and get your pockets picked, men. Or there are going to be *serious* consequences.

Were the "serious consequences" a hint of things to come if Michael and Showalter persisted in their brazen, reckless, virtually insubordinate brand of *competence?* Well, stubborn as they were, they did keep it up, and they thoughtlessly continued their efforts to build the foundation of a World Championship team. As a result they're no longer with the organization.

I hate Steinbrenner . . . for making intelligent trades more difficult by building his legacy of ever-escalating attempts to channel all baseball decisions through the lens of some personal animus or other.

61. Say, That's a Fascinating Idea—Tell Me More

"George has a favorite saying when he grudgingly accepts a suggestion from one of his underlings: 'All right,' George sneers, 'but this is on your head.' "
—*One of the boss's more endearing motivational techniques is revealed by George Vecsey, writing in the* New York Times.

Aren't you glad you don't work for this man? Don't you wish nobody did?

I wanted to talk for a moment about *why* George engages in this Stalinesque style of management. But you thought we should move on to the next entry and leave this one blank, rather than cite Steinbrenner's "possible fondness for causing coronaries among his employees' workplace pets."

Fine. I won't speculate for even a moment on whether or not the Boss takes a special joy in causing such high levels of stress among his underlings that he forces even little Flounder to forget to breathe deep through those tiny gills of his, silently repeat the words, "This too shall pass," and envision his master getting work somewhere else. I'm not going to write one single word about that. But if one more goldfish keels over and floats to the top of the bowl in someone's cubicle, it's on your head.

I hate Steinbrenner . . . for not recognizing that when you take a high-profile leadership position, it's on *your* head.

62. Did I Say That?

"I'm an involved guy. I never made any bones about it when I took over the Yankees. I said I'm going to be an involved owner."
  —*Steinbrenner during a* Sixty Minutes *interview with Harry Reasoner. Actually, when he took over the Yankees, he said exactly the opposite (see entry number two).*

Back in the early fifties, politicians used to tell a joke about Richard Nixon before he became president of the United States. They used to say that Nixon would lie when the truth would sound better. Then they used to rear back their heads and laugh. After a quarter century or so, when Nixon had been president for a while, a lot of politicians found themselves thinking about that joke and wondering whether or not it had really been that funny after all.

It seems a similar situation has arisen a quarter century or so into the Boss's reign.

Why would the Boss say something like this when there was clearly no earthly advantage to be gained from doing so? You've got me. One of the distinctive traits of the Steinbrenner era, to be sure, has been the Idiotic (and Transparent) Lie Told at the Expense of Another Person. But *another* distinctive trait of the Steinbrenner era has been the Idiotic—(and Transparent)—Lie Told For No Apparent Reason. We have here a sterling example of a lie in the latter category.

I hate Steinbrenner . . . for this and countless other "why bother" falsehoods that riddled the Yankee organization's credibility among fans and members of the media.

63. The Phantom Elevator Conflict

Remember this one?

Billy Martin sent a telegram to Steinbrenner after the Yankee owner was allegedly accosted in California between 1981 World Series games by two Los Angeles fans whom the Boss claimed badmouthed New York City. The telegram read as follows: "I understand exactly how you must have felt in that elevator. I only hope you don't have a good-behavior clause in your contract. By the way, the marshmallow man I hit was saying bad things about New York and the Yankees. Seriously, hope you are O.K. and good luck the next two games." (Martin once lost his job as Yankee manager over a fistfight with a marshmallow salesman.)

Other than the Boss himself, nobody ever saw these guys who supposedly attacked Steinbrenner. Did it really happen? Who knows? Ask yourself this question though: If *you'd* gotten into a fistfight with a multimillionaire, a fistfight to which there were no outside wit-

nesses, would *you* consider, just for the briefest moment, filing a civil suit for damages?

Some would argue that the much-discussed, unobserved conflict was the single most entertaining event of the strike-marred 1981 season—whether or not the scuffle actually took place. Others maintain that the event (or nonevent, as the case may be) was classic Steinbrenner media manipulation and as such simply represents more self-aggrandizing bilge from the Boss. Your humble correspondent has no direct knowledge of these events but inclines to the latter opinion.

I hate Steinbrenner . . . because he either lies about things like this to get headlines—*or* he has mystifyingly bad karma with strangers he encounters in elevators. (See next entry.)

64. When in Doubt About How to Break the Ice in an Unfamiliar Social Situation, Mouth Off to a Complete Stranger About How Much You Detest His Personal Appearance

Shades of Archie Bunker! En route to his Yankee Stadium office one day, Steinbrenner shared an elevator ride with a young man to whom he had never been introduced, a man who had unusually long hair. "Get a haircut," Steinbrenner sniped.

Nice to meet you, too, sir.

The fellow turned out to be running some errands for the *New York Times.* Oops.

Give the Boss credit. He's apparently profoundly concerned about These Kids Today. And maybe he was trying, in his own sledgehammer way, to warn the young man about the dangers of associating with the wrong crowd. You know. Nonconformists. People who hang out at the fringes of society. Gamblers attempting to peddle damaging information about highly paid outfielders, for instance.

What is it with this man and haircuts? As outlined elsewhere in this book, the Yankee Establishment's sacrosanct pronouncements concerning hair length made for some ludicrous headlines later on in the Steinbrenner era. Wouldn't you just love to turn up some long-suppressed photograph of George frolicking gaily with the hippie types during the Woodstock celebration with a Procul Harum record in one hand and an herbal jazz cigarette in the other? Don't you wish such a photograph existed? Wouldn't it have come in handy as potential blackmail material for the chance acquaintances (and Yankee players) who may have been accosted unexpectedly by the Boss on this issue over the years?

I hate Steinbrenner . . . because he has been known to treat total strangers just as badly as he treats the players on his big-league base-ball team.

65. The Fine Art of Second-Guessing and/or Humiliating One's Own Managers Through the Media (See also: Entries for Individual Managers Whose Life George Made a Living Managerial Hell)

Here's Steinbrenner's public assessment of Billy Martin during one of the latter's five—count 'em, five—stays at the helm: "He's the manager—until he screws up."

Although that demotivating quote above was aimed at a man with whom Steinbrenner nurtured a complex, neoabsurdist, quasi-codependent relationship over the years, it could just as easily have been launched in the direction of any number of skippers who passed through the revolving Yankee door since the Boss took over. The record-setting traffic in managers under Steinbrenner's watch has been notable not only for its freewheeling hirings and firings but also for its headline-grabbing public snipes, many obviously designed to make the life of the current Yankee skipper unbearable. Representative, and perhaps the most pathetic, of these prefiring rituals was the Boss's ongoing George-in-the-garden-of-Gethsemane routine for the press after manager Dick Howser's failure to move the Yankees past the Kansas City Royals in 1980 playoffs. Howser had guided the Yankees to their best regular-season record since 1963, but that wasn't enough to spare him public degradation in the tabloids. Howser eventually departed in a typically classless, Steinbrenner-orchestrated media event.

As of this writing, Joe Torre has yet to have his name dragged through the mud for guiding the Bronx Bombers to their first world championship since 1978. But is anyone willing to bet it couldn't and/or won't happen?

When you manage for George, part of the job description appears to be a willingness to accept humiliation, both public and private. Sometimes the public humiliation takes the form of verbal assaults that show up in the papers, up to and including public musings from the owner on whether or not you've been "outmanaged" in key contests. Sometimes the public humiliation takes the form of amateurishly bungled efforts at press relations, mistakes that are simply inexplicable after the Boss's long years of experience in dealing with the New York media. The mishandled departure of Buck Showalter in 1995 (chronicled elsewhere in this volume) serves as an example of this species of manager abuse.

Postscript: Dick Howser piloted the Kansas City Royals to a World Series championship in 1985.

I hate Steinbrenner . . . because he is single-handedly responsible for instituting a long-running series of media circuses around managerial control of what used to be the most stable and respected franchise in the history of American sport.

66. And for My Next Trick, I Will Offer, With a Straight Face, What Must Be the World's Least Convincing Rationalization to Be Happy About Having Been Fired as Manager of the New York Yankees

"Why would you want to stay manager and be second-guessed by me when you can come up into the front-office and be one of the second-guessers?"
—*Steinbrenner to the recently canned manager Gene Michael in 1981.*

Steinbrenner is an acknowledged master of the tactic of shuffling people around to "other jobs in the Yankee organization" as a consolation prize for having been publicly humiliated and forced out as Yankee manager. Titles change. Official duties change. The degree to which anyone other than Steinbrenner, in the final analysis, gets to "be one of the second-guessers" is, shall we say, open to debate.

It is true that Steinbrenner's all-too-short 1990 banishment from the game appears to have allowed team officials—including the much-traveled Gene Michael—a measure of *relative* autonomy, resulting in a core squad that managed to deliver great results in the mid-nineties, including the 1996 World Championship. With the Boss back on the job, however, it's a good bet that the heated "conferences" with Steinbrenner will continue. Bottom-line question: Would *you* want to report directly to this man?

Hey, it could have been worse. Steinbrenner could have turned around and given the manager's job back to Gene Michael again the next season, only to repeat the sad this-job's-not-right-for-the-man variations. No, wait a minute. He *did* turn around and give the manager's job back to Gene Michael again the next season, only to repeat the sad this-job's-not-right-for-the-man variations.

I hate Steinbrenner . . . because the predictable musical-chairs holocausts in the Yankee front office over the last two and a half decades have been flat-out bad for baseball.

67. I Don't Understand—Why Should We Have Held a Night in Buck Showalter's Honor on June 6, 1995, at Yankee Stadium?

"Obviously, it's a landmark. No question about that, and deservedly so."
  —*Dallas Green, on Showalter's passing Billy Martin as the Yankee manager to manage the most consecutive games under George Steinbrener. Showalter managed his 472nd straight game on June 6, 1995.*

And they say nothing in baseball will ever surpass Joe DiMaggio's 56-game hitting streak. The big event took place right under our noses, but somehow we never heard about it.

Move aside, Cal Ripken. Who cares about a *player's* consecutive-game streak? Players don't have to take regular calls from that volcano known as Mount George. Showalter did, and that should mean, in this writer's humble opinion, that every one of his games counts for *at least* five of the games in Ripken's streak.

Steinbrenner's mysterious decision not to launch a major promotional effort to celebrate Showalter's streak—perhaps a night in his honor at Yankee Stadium, with all the (living) former managers whom he eclipsed in respectful attendance lined up to shake his hand—must rank with Yeti, the Bermuda Triangle, and the continuing popularity of Michael Bolton as one of the great unanswered riddles of our time. For some unfathomable reason, Showalter's achievement went formally unrecognized by the Yankee organization.

Profounder puzzles would follow. One mystery: why this consummate team player and all-around standup guy would eventually be rewarded for his years of service by being hung out to dry in the press—immediately after leading the Yankees to their first postseason appearance in fourteen years. Another mystery: the motives behind Steinbrenner's bizarre postseparation attempts at reconciliation with his rejected manager.

Mysteries abound in the world of the Boss. Next week: the Loch Ness Monster.

Stability? What's stability? Did it ever have anything to do with the New York Yankees? Who can remember nowadays? Granted, the Boss didn't exactly *invent* habitual mistreatment of managers, but he seems to have perfected it in the current era. His failure to publicly acknowledge the commitment, patience, and, yes, longevity of the ever-suffering Showalter was an inexplicable lapse.

As a point of comparison, note that Miller Huggins started the season as Yankee manager for twelve straight years, Joe McCarthy for sixteen straight years, and Casey Stengel for twelve straight years.

I hate Steinbrenner . . . because he's forgotten a big part of what made the "old" Yankees great—*decade-long* front-office partnerships with a single manager.

68. That Steadily More Pathetic Vaudeville Routine With Billy Martin

"One's a born liar and the other's convicted."
> —*Billy Martin's famous 1978 remark to the press about Reggie Jackson and George Steinbrenner. The ill-advised crack led to Martin's inaugural dismissal as Yankee manager. In the first of several high-profile Steinbrenner/Martin reconciliations, Martin's scheduled return to the Yankees was announced the same year.*

"Billy Martin has been relieved of his duties as manager of the New York Yankees and Dick Howser has been named to succeed him effective immediately."
> —*October 1979 statement to the press from Steinbrenner after the rehired Martin was revealed to have been engaged in a barroom brawl with a marshmallow salesman. Really.*

"This will be different, because Billy and I will communicate better with each other."

> —*Steinbrenner to the press, announcing Martin's third stint as manager in 1983. Apparently they didn't.*

"We have never been closer."

> —*Steinbrenner to the press, announcing Martin's fourth stint as manager in 1985. Apparently they weren't all that close after all. Steinbrenner eventually dismissed Martin and named Lou Piniella as manager.*

"Martin, back for the fifth time as manager, [got] beaten up in a topless bar and [was] subsequently fired again."

> —*Bill Madden and Moss Klein on the 1988 New York Yankees season, a year best filed under "long, strange trip."*

Billy made headlines on his own. Billy made headlines when George fired him. Billy made headlines when George hired him again. What's not to like? Chaos is good for the system, right?

George probably tells himself that Martin's own unfortunate, increasingly rapid, alcohol-fueled decline can be cited as sufficient justification for each of his dismissals. George is probably right. George would also probably like to think of himself as the man who gave Billy his second, third, fourth, and fifth chances. One wonders though whether or not the Boss questions himself about how his highly public, highly dysfunctional relationship with Martin may have made the manager's descent quicker and more inglorious than it had to be. One wonders too about how deeply Martin considered the possibility that his name was being exploited as a means of bringing fans into Yankee Stadium.

Sure, Billy Martin was a grown-up responsible for his own decisions. Sure, he was a man with a problem. But the question remains: Why did Billy Martin have to be put through the wringer at Yankee Stadium as often as he was? One thing is certain: The "Billy's back and this time it's going to be different" charade got steadily more difficult for fans—or anyone else—to take seriously. But Martin's desire to win the skipper's job for good was something he appears to have taken seriously all the way to the end of the line.

Billy Martin got very old very quickly—in part, of course, because of his fondness for spirituous beverages. It's fair to observe, though, that his neverending scuffles with the Boss didn't do his outlook on life much good either.

The Baseball Encyclopedia reports that Billy Martin, as a player, compiled a .333 lifetime batting average in the World Series and that he was a regular for the Yankees during some of their very best years (1950–1960), compiling a .257 regular season average and scoring a total of 425 runs. It also reports that as a manager he piloted Yankee squads to two World Series appearances and won one of them, the Fall Classic victory of 1977. What it doesn't list is the number of times the man almost went nuts trying to get George Steinbrenner to let him skipper the Bronx Bombers on a full-time basis *after* that World Series victory. Nobody knows the actual number, but it was too high. His run-ins with George after that extraordinary season always seemed to leave Billy looking worse for wear and tear. They weren't the *only* things that left him looking worse for wear and tear, of course. But it would be a bald-faced lie to say that problems with George weren't high on the list. If he was never going to win the post full time, it might have been better for everyone if he'd been kept, well, out of the rotation (as it were).

Is it surprising that Billy lost his edge during the eighties? No. It *is* a little surprising, however, that Steinbrenner seems to have had (and perhaps still has) no clue about the effect the whole "when's-he-getting-canned-next" game may have had on his troubled skipper's exploits both on and off the field.

I hate Steinbrenner . . . because although Steinbrenner's relationship with Martin seems to fall into the dark, stormy category that is often euphemistically referred to as "complex," it's certainly hard to deny that the Boss played *some* role in stoking one of baseball's least appealing ongoing stories: the one that splashed across tabloid pages in huge headlines during Martin's second through fifth tenures as manager of the Yankees.

69. Dick Howser's Life Turns Into a Living Managerial Hell

"I'm certainly not going to walk away from the ballclub."

That's what Yankee manager Dick Howser said to reporters in 1980 after the Yankees, winners of 103 regular season games—the team's best regular-season finish since 1964—were upset by the Kansas City Royals in the playoffs.

"Dick has decided that he will not be returning to the Yankees next year. I should say, not returning to the Yankees as manager."

That's how George Steinbrenner announced Howser's change of heart for him in November, 1980. Which brings us to . . .

"I'm not going to comment."

That's how Howser responded to the question, "Were you fired?" posed at the same press conference at which Steinbrenner made his announcement. Eight months later Howser later ended his strange, seemingly involuntary Florida real estate career and accepted the job of manager of the Kansas City Royals. He eventually led that team to its first World Series title in 1985.

If *you* took over as manager after a chaotic 1979 season and posted the team's best won-lost record in two decades, would you think you had a shot at coming back the next year? Would you think you had some say in the coaches you'd be working with? You would? Think again.

Never forget! The slaughterhouse personnel system Steinbrenner developed applies even to *winning* Yankee managers like Howser.

I hate Steinbrenner . . . because he not only instituted the whole rotating-manager travesty in the first place, he tried to treat Howser, a fine manager, as though he were Charlie McCarthy.

70. Bob Lemon's Life Turns Into a Living Managerial Hell

"Bob Lemon is going to be our manager all year. You can bet on it. I don't care if we come in last. I swear on my heart he'll be the manager all season. That's all he wants, one full season, and then he wants to go back to Southern California, and I owe him that much."

—*Steinbrenner before the 1982 season on Hall of Famer Bob Lemon, who was fired after a slow start and replaced by Gene Michael. Michael himself yielded to Clyde King, and the Yankees stumbled to a fifth-place finish.*

Lemon, a previous firee as Yankee manager, was let go when the season was only fourteen games old.

Do you see a pattern emerging here?

I hate Steinbrenner . . . because the whole terrify-the-manager-of-the-month thing he pulled with Lemon got really old, really quick. (But keep reading. It's not over yet, not by a longshot.)

71. Gene Michael's Life Turns Into a Living Managerial Hell

"I don't think it's right that I should constantly be threatened by him and yelled at in front of my coaches. He can take the job, but he's not gonna bring me down."
> —*Not long after Gene Michael made these remarks to the press, he was removed as Yankee manager.*

In 1981 Michael earned the unusual distinction of having been fired after he guided the Yankees into the playoffs (they had clinched a spot as a result of their finish before the player's strike in the 1981 season) but *before* the team actually engaged in postseason play. Under Clyde King the Bronx Bombers won the American League pennant but lost to the Los Angeles Dodgers in the World Series. Michael came back as manager—for a while—in 1982.

Years later, as general manager, Michael was *again* ousted (with manager Buck Showalter) after he'd helped to fashion the nucleus of the Yankee squad that returned to contention in the mid-nineties . . . and copped the World Championship in 1996.

I hate Steinbrenner . . . because the remarkably resilient Michael should have gotten a heck of a lot more respect from the Boss during his stint as manager.

72. (This Is a Biggie) Yogi Berra's Life Turns Into a Living Managerial Hell

"Yogi will be the manager the entire season, win or lose."
  —*Steinbrenner in February of 1985.*

"The level of play dictated a change had to be made."
  —*Steinbrenner's justification for sacking Berra just sixteen games into the regular season.*

"[S]ince his dismissal as manager 10 years ago, [Yogi Berra] has stuck to his vow never to return to Yankee Stadium as long as Steinbrenner owns the Yankees."

The Yankees' 6–10 start apparently was too much for the Boss to take. Or maybe it was the fact that people, you know, liked Yogi Berra a lot more than some other people in the organization we might name.

This was probably Steinbrenner's single most pointless, inexcusable ego-driven power trip—and that's saying something. Simply put, Yogi Berra, a Yankee immortal, a Hall of Famer, *and a pre-Steinbrenner-era pennant-winning manager* (1964) did not deserve what he got at the hands of the Boss in 1985. What's more, baseball as a whole did not deserve what happened to Yogi Berra at the hands of George Steinbrenner. If the Boss had had a clue, he'd have been ashamed of himself. He didn't, so he wasn't.

When Yankee players protested the senseless firing, Steinbrenner suggested Berra's departure was *the players'* fault for not winning more games under Berra. (Again, folks, the ax fell *sixteen games into the 1985 season*, and Berra had posted a winning season the year before.)

Before we conclude this entry, a few observations on Berra's utterly justified boycott of Yankee Stadium are in order. First and foremost, wouldn't it be a potent symbol if the Boss threw an old-timer's game and *nobody* came? Just a thought for the veterans in the crowd if you get my meaning. Second, note Yogi's canny continuance of the boycott throughout Steinbrenner's supposedly "permanent" separation from the Yankees in 1990. The man's no dummy, friends. This voluntary exile retains that special, detached wariness of a man Who Knows What's Up. When he was asked about the long-term prospects of Steinbrenner's supposed "breakthrough" manager, Buck Showalter—he who managed for three whole years in a row, got the team back into contention, and was summarily shown the door—Berra copped a "wait and see" approach. This is all by way of saying what Yogi has known for some time . . . that it ain't over till it's over. And we'll know right away when the bad old days of King George are over. When Yogi says they're over, they'll be over.

While we're waiting, with Yogi, for the Boss era to come to a close, let's note that Berra's courageous decision to skip Yankee Stadium playoff and World Series games, days in his honor, and all the rest, stands as the starkest, most fitting judgment on the last tumultuous quarter century of New York Yankee history. May the boycott conclude, on Berra's own stated terms, in the very near future.

Sell the team please, George. We want to see Yogi where he belongs.

I hate Steinbrenner . . . because firing Yogi Berra ranks as one of the most disgraceful episodes in New York Yankee history.

73. Lou Piniella's Life Turns Into a Living Managerial Hell

"The simple fact is [Lou] Piniella didn't even come back from lunch—if that was where he really was—to get a call from his boss at two o'clock. He didn't bother to call me or to get word to me that the time was inconvenient for him."
> —*From Steinbrenner's 1987 press statement lambasting his own manager for missing a phone call. Not surprisingly, the statement made front-page news.*

"If that was where he really was." Don't you love the dark implication at work in this carefully crafted bit of media-accessible smear work? If you were a sports reporter working in New York, would you be able to resist the notion of being able to tell your readers, via a direct quote, that the principal owner of the New York Yankees was on the record as harboring vague suspicions that the team's manager was involved in some discreetly unnamed nefarious activity or other? If you were *reading* the papers the next morning, wouldn't you wonder whether or not Steinbrenner thought Piniella had somehow been linked to late-breaking developments in the Alger Hiss case or the leak of the Pentagon Papers or something?

Surprise, surprise: Lou's days as Yankee manager were numbered.

For some inexplicable reason, he agreed to take the helm as skipper once again in 1988, so his days as Yankee manager could be numbered all over again.

Postscript: Lou Piniella guided the Cincinnati Reds to a four-game sweep of the heavily favored Oakland Athletics in the 1990 World Series. That same year the Yankees posted their worst season since 1913.

I hate Steinbrenner . . . because he made sure Piniella had more reasons than the Count of Monte Cristo to nurse a long-term grudge.

74. Dallas Green's Life Turns Into a Living Managerial Hell

"Dallas Green . . . will be there the whole year. You can mark it down."
   —*Steinbrenner to the press in July of 1989. Green was fired the following month.*

Do you get the feeling that the worst possible thing that can happen to you if you're named to manage the New York Yankees is to have George Steinbrenner promise he's not going to fire you?

Steinbrenner referred to his decision to hire Dallas Green as "one of the biggest mistakes I ever made," apparently unaware of the intense competition in that category. After he'd been fired, Green decided to let it all hang out and share his unique personal insights on the Steinbrenner style. "George doesn't know a f___ing thing about the game of baseball," Green opined. "That's the bottom line."

I hate Steinbrenner . . . because as Green might put it, the Boss doesn't know a f___ing thing about working with big-league managers, and that's the bottom line.

75. Will the Next Man Into the Lion's Den Please Stand When His Number Is Called?

"If you ain't got a hernia yet, you ain't pulling your share of the load."
    —*Sign spotted in Steinbrenner's office in 1990.*

If Bucky Dent didn't have a hernia before he was named Yankee manager in 1989, he may well have thought he had one when he was fired in 1990. Dent, the unlikely hero of the 1978 World Championship season, became the latest in a series of former Yankee "name" players to be lured into the manager's job, generate a few "entrance" headlines, spark some fan interest, manage for a spell, and then generate a few "exit" headlines. Yogi Berra, Billy Martin, and Lou Piniella all got caught in the same snare. "Pulling one's load" for the Yankees apparently means allowing George to cash in on one's name for as long as the whim moves him.

So. Why do people *take* this job? People take this job because, no matter how irrationally George acts, and no matter how much they know about how horrifically he treats people, *it's still managing the New York Yankees.* And hey, who knows. You might just win the Series, as Joe Torre did. Then again, you might get shuffled off to big-league oblivion, as Dent did.

P.S.: As of this writing, no one has offered Dent another big-league managing job.

Steinbrenner's occasional and utterly ill-informed fixation on the publicity associated with hiring and firing "big Yankee name" managers—the same obsession that seems to have fueled the sad Billy Martin charade—reveals him as an opportunistic manipulator.

I hate Steinbrenner . . . because he named Bucky Dent as manager long before Dent was ready for the job.

76. Today's Trivia Question—Who's Gone Through More Big-League Managers Than George Steinbrenner?

Okay, time's up. The answer, of course, is nobody. Here's the sad, record-setting chronology:

1973: Ralph Houk steps down as Yankee manager after the season concludes. He is eventually succeeded by Bill Virdon.

104 games into the 1975 season: Bill Virdon is out, and Billy Martin is in.

94 games into the 1978 season: Billy Martin loses his job for calling Steinbrenner "convicted." Bob Lemon takes over.

96 games into the 1979 season: Bob Lemon is out. Billy Martin is back in again.

Author's note: The rehiring of Martin marks the beginning of the "revolving-door" management cycle for Steinbrenner's New York Yankees. It is a cycle that produces . . . shall we say . . . mixed results on the field.

October 1979: Billy Martin is out again, after having gotten into a fight with a marshmallow salesman. Dick Howser takes over.

November 1980: Steinbrenner announces Dick Howser's strangely unconvincing decision to step down as manager of the Yankees. Gene Michael eventually signs on as skipper.

September 1981: Steinbrenner fires Gene Michael and rehires Bob Lemon.

April 1982: Steinbrenner fires Bob Lemon and rehires Gene Michael.

August 1982: Steinbrenner fires Gene Michael again and hires Clyde King as interim skipper.

January 1983: Steinbrenner fires Clyde King and hires Billy Martin for the third time.

December 1983: Steinbrenner fires Billy Martin for the third time and hires Yogi Berra.

April 1985: Steinbrenner fires Yogi Berra and hires Billy Martin for the fourth time.

October 1985: Steinbrenner fires Billy Martin for the fourth time and hires Lou Piniella.

October 1987: Steinbrenner fires Lou Piniella and hires Billy Martin for the fifth time.

Author's note: The previous entry does not reflect a typographical error. Piniella was allowed to manage the Yankees for the 1986 and 1987 seasons. This mysterious portion of the record may be traceable to an administrative error of some kind in the Yankee front office during the period in question. Current scholarship has not yet developed the tools necessary to develop a more convincing explanation for this odd disruption of the normally reliable Steinbrenner firing patterns.

June 1988: Steinbrenner fires Billy Martin for the fifth time and rehires Lou Piniella.

October 1988: Steinbrenner fires Lou Piniella and hires Dallas Green.

August 1989: Steinbrenner fires Dallas Green and hires Bucky Dent.

June 1990: Steinbrenner fires Bucky Dent and hires Stump Merrill.

During the 1990 season Steinbrenner is forced to yield control of the Yankees as a result of consorting with gambler Howie Spira. Despite the banishment, the front office manages to can Stump Merrill the following year, presumably in an attempt to keep up appearances with Yankees fans, who have come to expect an average of at least one managerial firing per season.

And then there was Buck Showalter.

After Steinbrenner's formal (and supposedly permanent) exile as boss of the New York Yankees concluded in 1993, he found himself looking at a new beginning. Once Steinbrenner resumed control of the club, he could deal openly with Showalter, who turned out to be the kind of manager who might—just might—be able to handle the Boss's eccentricities and *still* find a way to field a winning ballclub. The transformation seemed complete in 1994, when the Yankees occupied first place in the American League East at the time the player strike cut off the season—and the playoffs. Then in 1995 Showalter guided the Yankees into the wild-card slot. The Bronx Bombers were back in postseason play at last, for the first time since 1981.

It really had worked. With a good manager and a sound front-office effort headed up by managerial-revolving-door alumnus Gene Michael, the Yankees had turned things around.

Surely, the fans of New York must have thought to themselves, the worst aspects of the bad old days were now over. Surely Steinbrenner remembered all too well what the chaos and instability of the 1980s had brought the once-proud franchise—a series of nervous breakdowns and the bitter memory of the 1990 season, the team's worst since 1913. Surely the boss preferred 1995 to 1990. Surely he would find a way to work with the tactful, ever-patient, team-oriented Showalter. And even if Steinbrenner fell victim to his darker side, surely he would find a way to let Showalter go without humiliating him in person or via the media.

If that's what Yankee fans thought, they were wrong. Halfway into the nineties, George Steinbrenner reverted to classic eighties form and found a nice, classless way to get rid of Buck Showalter. (See the next entry.)

Joe Torre, the man who would bring the Yankees their first World Series title since the Billy Martin days, was in. That, it turned out, was the good news. But the all-too-predictable bad news was that his predecessor had been (ready for a shocker?) treated like dirt.

I hate Steinbrenner . . . because he committed the single most unpardonable sin of our era: failing to learn anything from the 1980s.

77. A Surprised Buck Showalter Learns From the Media That He Has Voluntarily Stepped Down

"The Yankees announced an hour before the start of the fifth game of the World Series that [Buck] Showalter, whose three-year contract expires next Tuesday, told the owner today that he would not return for 1996. But about two hours after the Yankees' announcement, Showalter said he was not aware he had resigned."

—*The manager who put up with it all gets some bad news . . . while under the impression his contract negotiations were still in process.*

"We tried but were unable to dissuade Buck. . . . I am very upset by his leaving. I wish Buck and his fine little family nothing but the best. There will be no criticism of Buck in any way from me."

—*Steinbrenner tries to paper over the pesky details surrounding his manager's "decision" to step down.*

We all thought he couldn't top himself in the "getting-the-manager-out-the-door" category, but we were wrong. Once the Boss had finally found a manager who would maintain a discreet relationship that had no place for "disloyalty" via on-the-record comments to the press, a manager who actually showed signs of being able to put up with the innumerable "I'm-in-charge" phone tirades, a manager who even went so far to refer to the Yankee owner as "Mr. Steinbrenner" rather than "George"—what did the Great Boat Builder do? He bungled the man's exit from the scene. Fine payment for a skipper who had led the Yankees back to postseason play for the first time in nearly a decade and a half. By the way, all this happened while the rest of the baseball establishment was trying to get fans to focus on the first World Series since the 1994 strike debacle. George grabbed headlines during this critical period, thus further wounding an already incapacitated National Pastime.

Wait till November to launch another soap opera? Why? Was there a problem last year with the fans?

But the story gets even more unbelievable.

I hate Steinbrenner . . . because the Showalter heave-ho proved that the "bad old days" of George's humiliate-the-manager act hadn't really ended after all.

78. Let Us Now Gracelessly Break Up the Braintrust That Assembled the Yankees' First Squad to Make the Playoffs in a Decade and a Half

"It didn't matter that the Yanks went 26–7 down the stretch to make the playoffs for the first time since 1981; [Buck] Showalter was gone, and so was GM Gene Michael."
  —*Gordon Edes, writing in the* Fort Lauderdale Sun-Sentinel *during spring training 1996, shines a light on the latest mysterious front-office move.*

Bye-bye Buck. Bye-bye Gene.

You might *think* that steady improvement and the development of a playoff-level team would solidify your job with the Yankees. But then, after having parted company with George, you'd recall the fates of people who managed to bring the team within two games of first place, but didn't get a shot the next season (Billy Martin, 1985), who won the division title, but didn't get a shot the next season (Dick Howser, 1980), who clinched a spot in the playoffs, but who didn't get to finish the *same* season (Gene Michael, 1981), who won the American League Championship Series, but didn't make it past April of the next season (Bob Lemon, 1981), who won the World Series, but didn't make it past July of the next season (Billy Martin, 1977—admittedly a special case, but, hey, it happened).

When will people learn? You get fired for *losing* for George. And you also get fired for *winning* for George. You'd probably also get fired for finishing at exactly .500 for George, although no one's tried that yet.

I hate Steinbrenner . . . because Gene Michael and Buck Showalter were superior baseball men who'd put up with enough not to have to be subjected to the "you-won-now-get-out-of-here" syndrome.

79. The Secret of My Success? Superior People Skills, of Course.

"Did Steinbrenner visit Showalter in his hometown of Pensacola, Florida, three or four days after Joe Torre was appointed on Nov. 2 and offer the former manager the seemingly unfathomable chance to return to guide the Yankees? 'I don't think I have any comment on that,' Showalter said. 'That's not fair to Joe. Don't get that going. It's dead. It's not fair to Joe. It wasn't exactly like that at all.' According to a person within the major-league base-ball community, it was exactly like that, and according to an American League official, it was almost like that. . . . Steinbrenner did not return telephone calls seeking comment on his meeting with Showalter."

   —*Reports circulate that the boss made a surrealistic appeal to get Showalter to consider rejoining the organization shortly after utterly mismanaging Showalter's departure.*

Could it really have taken place? The *New York Times* seemed to think so. The idea appears to have been to use Showalter as a backup in case the Joe Torre thing didn't work out. Showalter could have agreed to the idea. Fortunately he had the sense not to.

   Doesn't this scheme of Steinbrenner's remind you just a little of the long-running Billy Martin cycle, in which Steinbrenner assigned particular years to a series of managers, then failed to follow his own plan? Are you surprised that Showalter apparently didn't jump at the chance to reawaken that esteemed tradition?

I hate Steinbrenner . . . because the sheer outrageousness of making an offer like this after Showalter had been hung out to dry in the local press leaves the mind reeling at the Boss's shamelessness.

80. I Am Julius Caesar

"For him to say there are no hard feelings is like Brutus telling Julius Caesar there are no hard feelings after he stabbed him."
—*Steinbrenner reacting to catcher Rick Cerone's conciliatory remarks after the catcher had won a salary arbitration case in 1981.*

Classical persecution complexes, anyone? Was it the highfalutin' Roman reference or the tone of surrealistically inappropriate self-pity that made this remark such a memorable George-ism? Who knows. One thing's for certain, though. When the Boss lets loose with a "to-whom-shall-I-compare-myself" sound bite, he goes with a real whopper.

Cerone was the one who responded less than charitably to a dressing-down Steinbrenner delivered after a Yankee loss to the Milwaukee Brewers in the 1981 playoffs. For those who'd like a brief recap of the discussion with Rick Cerone (and isn't that all of us?), the Yankee catcher's answer to the Boss's latest diatribe about the team's many shortcomings was as follows: "F___ you, George."

Et tu, Brute?

The Boss may well have been warming up for a role in an upcoming amateur Shakespeare production rich in unintentional irony. The records on this are unclear, however, and no reliable contemporary reference to Steinbrenner having portrayed the Bard's aging, self-absorbed tyrant-in-waiting have come down to us.

(By the way, it gets worse. See the next entry.)

I hate Steinbrenner . . . for publicly comparing himself to the legendary Roman general without the slightest trace of shame or insight.

81. I Am Abraham Lincoln

"You think Lincoln was popular? . . . Lincoln said, 'I do the very best I can. If the end brings me out right, what is said against me won't amount to anything. If the end brings me out wrong, ten angels swearing I was right would make no difference.' I have that saying up in my office, at Yankee Stadium, everywhere."
—*Steinbrenner invokes the memory of the nation's greatest president.*

You know, when you think about it, the connections really *are* remarkable. One guy was struggling to keep the Union from falling apart while coordinating the military struggle against those who embraced slavery of their fellow human beings. The other guy was running full speed from the office of the commissioner of baseball because he'd consorted with a gambler who was peddling dirt on a star player. Yeah. It all makes sense to me now. Steinbrenner really *was* facing a very similar situation to the one Lincoln faced during the Civil War.
    Not.
    As is made clear elsewhere in this book, some of Steinbrenner's pronouncements lead one to wonder just how familiar he is with the most enduring legacies of the man from Illinois, the Emancipation Proclamation, and the Thirteenth Amendment to the $%$# Constitution of the United States.

I hate Steinbrenner . . . for publicly comparing himself to the Great Emancipator without the slightest trace of shame or insight.

82. I Am Napoleon Bonaparte

In early '93, he really did dress up as the Corsican dictator for *Sports Illustrated,* but the parallel went only so far. The real-life Napoleon eventually *stayed* exiled, a distinctly positive outcome that has yet to materialize in Steinbrenner's case.

The real-life Napoleon also observed, "All celebrated people lose dignity on close view." Don't they though?

I hate Steinbrenner . . . for failing to find a permanent spot for his exile.

83. I Am the Monarch of the Sea, the Ruler of the Queen's Na-Vee

"Keep in mind, keep in mind, there's only one admiral on this ship. There may be some vice-admirals, but only one admiral. So let's get out there and have some fun!!!"
   —*Steinbrenner reassuring the 1986 New York Yankees during a bizarre team meeting called to announce a truce between himself and Yankee player rep Dave Winfield over the issue of drug testing.*

Anchors aweigh. Don't you feel motivated now?

Now that we all know who's in charge (and who's capable of making thoroughly inappropriate nautical references) we can all get out there and enjoy ourselves.

I hate Steinbrenner . . . for his inability to back off and let someone else steer the ship (a key character trait for most admirals)—and for comparing himself to Navy bigshots without the slightest trace of shame.

84. I Am George S. Patton

In the August 6, 1990, issue of *Newsweek,* Steinbrenner held forth on his management style: "I'm more of a Patton than an Eisenhower in the way I lead."

Don't you feel a certain grudging admiration for the guy, simply for his ability to cling, with unending tenacity, to a series of such ludicrously inappropriate self-descriptions? Isn't the level of cluelessness necessary to make remarks like these somehow awe-inspiring? Wouldn't you expect that the whole immortal-figures-from-history-thing would get embarrassing after a while?

By the way, General George S. Patton is on record as having said, "Never tell people how to do things. Tell them *what* to do and they will surprise you with their ingenuity." There's a classic Steinbrenner management principle for you.

Sorry, George. Stern, effective, and demanding leadership is not to be confused with consistently uninformed, frequently deceptive, and perpetually unaccountable leadership.

Who's next? Saint Francis of Assisi? Albert Schweitzer? Henry V?

I hate Steinbrenner . . . for publicly comparing himself to Old Blood and Guts without the slightest trace of shame.

85. Don Mattingly? "Selfish."

The Boss got down on first baseman Don Mattingly for being "selfish" after the star hit eight homers in eight consecutive games in 1987. The Yankee slugger hurt his wrist not long after this record-tying feat, and Steinbrenner chalked that up to Mattingly's "exaggerated home run swing."

You do have to watch out for those exaggerated home run swings, you know. They're a sign of extreme selfishness, and hitters who are on white-hot power streaks should never indulge in them. Too many of those exaggerated home run swings have been known to put exaggerated numbers of runs on the board for the team.

These are the kinds of accusations *nine-year-olds* make about players they don't like anymore because they traded away the relevant baseball cards in a fit of pique. They're not the public pronouncements one expects to read in black and white from a club owner—especially from one attempting, for his own mysterious reasons, to demonstrate his leadership qualities to fans, members of the media, and big-league ballplayers.

One wonders how Steinbrenner would have responded during Roger Maris's 61-homer season in 1961 or during Babe Ruth's 60-

homer performance in 1927. Doubtless the Boss would consider Hank Aaron to be the most selfish player in major-league history, given his undeniable habit of letting loose with exaggerated home run swings.

I hate Steinbrenner . . . because of the sheer absurdity and all-around baseball ignorance inherent in an accusation like this, and because it's not the only time he lambasted a respected star player for supposed "selfishness." (See next entry.)

86. Dave Winfield? "Selfish."

"The most selfish athlete I've ever known."
  —*Steinbrenner's assessment of Dave Winfield.*

We all know that Steinbrenner's fixation on Winfield appeared to border on the psychopathic, which means that, for all we know, he may not have been in complete rational control of his actions at all times. (That's a layman talking about when someone *looks* like he's gone off the deep end—I'll leave the clinical diagnosis to the experts.) All the same, he really shouldn't have gone out on a limb about how "selfish" the outfielder was. Not when the Boss was the one instigating the Hatfield-and-McCoy routine and keeping up contacts with gamblers, the better to develop material with which to smear Winfield. *Somebody's* ego got the better of him and led to big, big trouble during the Winfield years. Was it Dave's ego? Or someone else's?

Now, Steinbrenner *could* have made a classic Freudian slip of the tongue and referred to Winfield as "the most selfish player I ever *attempted to publicly humiliate for daring to defy my own bungling attempts to control matters about which I appear, for all the world, to know nothing."* It was a lucky thing he didn't say *that*.

I hate Steinbrenner . . . because this hamhanded, pseudoauthoritarian claptrap was just as embarrassing to the Yankee organization as the equally lamebrained attack on Mattingly.

87. Gimme, Gimme

The *Boston Globe* reported that "George Steinbrenner . . . had the consummate chutzpah to whine a few weeks back about how the Orioles have the revenue-generating potential of all those luxury boxes, while he's stuck in antiquated Yankee Stadium. Excuse me, Boss, but what about your $500 million local TV contract? I do believe the Orioles would swap broadcast deals."
    —*George's long-time observers can only shake their heads in dumbfounded amazement at his "poor-little-me" posturing.*

Times are tough, to hear George talk. When fans don't show up, he criticizes them through the media. When he's feeling as though he ought to be able to squeeze some more cash from his facilities, he pines for the financial advantages of parks other franchises have built (as evidenced previously) and threatens to leave historic Yankee Stadium, despite a gargantuan broadcasting contract small-market clubs would kill for.

For his shameless, unceasing, and endlessly showcased personal greed, and his severely limited "loyalty" (a favorite and oft-cited Steinbrenner virtue) to the fans of New York, the Boss gets the big, fat skunk-eye.

I hate Steinbrenner . . . because, after having landed a broadcast contract that is the envy of organized baseball, he has the unmitigated gall to complain about how little money he's making on the New York Yankees.

88. Which Raises the Question . . . Is There Perhaps Another Member of the Yankee Family to Whom the Word *Selfish* Might More Accurately Apply?

"George Steinbrenner has one simple ambition in life. He wants to own all the land next to his."
—*Pitcher Dan Quisenberry sums it all up nicely.*

"It's always how we're embarrassing ourselves and embarrassing New York and baseball and the country. George tells us how he was a football coach, and how he was in locker rooms before we were born. It's always 'I' this and 'I' that."
—*Catfish Hunter on George Steinbrenner's memorable pep talks.*

Catfish was right. All through the day, George's favorite Beatles song is on display: "I, me, mine." If there's a baseball owner who refers to his favorite subject—himself—more frequently, more ludicrously, or more consistently than George Steinbrenner, that owner certainly has yet to leave the impressive paper trail the Boss has over the past twenty-five years. Play along at home—and count the personal pronouns per square inch!

"*I* didn't fire the man. *I* think it's safe to say Dick Howser wants to be a Florida resident the year round."
—*Steinbrenner to the press in 1980, putting words into the mouth of the departing Dick Howser, who, at the very same press conference, refused to comment on whether or not he had been fired.*

"*I've* had it up to here with him. He's got to be the boss of everything."
—*Steinbrenner's own shrewd 1981 assessment of Reggie Jackson. As we all know, there's simply no room in the Yankee organization for that type of behavior from anyone.*

"*I'm* the boss, *I'm* the leader."
—*Steinbrenner to the press in 1981 during his run-ins with embattled manager Gene Michael.*

"*I* pay the bills around here. *I'll* say whatever *I* want."
—*Steinbrenner's 1981 response to catcher Rick Cerone's profane dismissal of a postgame tirade from the Boss.*

"If *I* were Lee MacPhail, *I'd* go house-hunting in Kansas City."
> —*Steinbrenner to the press in 1983, assailing the president of the American League for his actions relating to the "pine tar game."*

"You got *me* in there for two hours yesterday, *I* got you in there for three hours today."
> —*Is there a better way to spend the day than talking to opposing counsel? Steinbrenner's 1984 taunt to Dave Winfield as the Boss played dueling depositions over the Yankee boss's past commitments to pay money to the slugger's charitable fund.*

"What did [Gabe Paul] ever win before he worked with *me?*"
> —*Steinbrenner on the man who helped make the 1977 and 1978 championships a reality.*

"*I'm* the leader. *I'm* the admiral."
> —*Steinbrenner during a 1985 run-in with Dave Winfield.*

"*I'm* hardest on the people *I* feel closest to."
> —*Steinbrenner explaining his inscrutable motivational techniques to Winfield.*

"*I'll* win. I always do."
> —*Steinbrenner apparently referring to his personal struggles with the commissioner's office, not the dismal performance of his ballclub during the 1990 season.*

"I don't care. I will deal with it in my own way. I haven't softened. *I'm* just as tough as *I* was before."
> —*Steinbrenner on leading the Yankees of 1995.*

But it's not as though he's "selfish" or anything. That label is reserved for players like Winfield and Mattingly. Right?

It's as though George is afraid the words "I" and "me" lose their meaning if not used every thirty seconds or so—ideally, to accuse someone else of wrongdoing or to settle one of his perpetual feuds. Couple this fascinating conversational tic with his amply demonstrated massive personal greed and you get someone who could accurately be described as . . . gee, it beats me.

What a marvelous day it would be if the world famous Steinbrenner fault-finding mechanism were somehow turned, just for the shortest span of time, on the Boss himself. Might he, in a defining moment of personal insight, notice the barest *trace* evidence of selfishness on his own part and commit to a kick-the-habit program?

Hey, we can dream, can't we?

I hate Steinbrenner . . . for failing to realize that the best step to take, if he really wants to find the most appropriate target for his familiar accusation of "selfishness," is to consult the nearest mirror.

89. No Tricky Stuff, Pal

"Frisky American League hitters beware. Essentially, that was the message George Steinbrenner was sending when he ordered Manager Buck Showalter to request that umpires confiscate Tony Phillips's bat on Sunday before the first pitch of a game that the

Yankees won, 11–3, from the California Angels. The American League determined yesterday that the bat was clean and legal."
—*Something must have gone wrong with George's hot tip about that bat.*

Basically, and as a general operating principle, George suspects that something's up. And he wants his managers to do something about it.

Evidence that the man is convinced the world is out to cheat him isn't really all that hard to come by, and baseball should have built up something of an immunity to it by now. And let's not forget: Paranoia, consciously channeled toward as many supposedly devious opponents as possible, was the winning strategy for the Master of San Clemente.

Wasn't it?

In Steinbrenner's world people fall into two categories: enemies and underlings. Neither role is much fun to play. Woe unto you if the Boss gets it into his head that you're part of the Giant Plot That Is the Rest of the World. Woe unto you if you are selected to carry out the campaign meant to neutralize the Giant Plot That Is the Rest of the World.

I wonder if he apologized to the Angels.

I hate Steinbrenner . . . because he makes managers follow his own hunches, and because, more often than not, his hunches are wrong.

90. How to Use the Yankee Stadium Public Address System to Humiliate the Manager

What motivated the Boss to give away tickets after a doubleheader loss? Saintly generosity to the fans perhaps? It's hard to say because George wasn't doing a whole lot of explaining after this strange event.

"I will answer no questions." That was Steinbrenner's brushoff to the press on August 4, 1982, after announcing, during a 1:00 A.M. press conference, Gene Michael's second firing as Yankee manager. (Answering no questions except those that suit him is an old weapon in his press relations arsenal, one that he continues to use to this day.)

The announcement immediately followed a pair of Yankee losses to the Chicago White Sox. During the second game of the doubleheader, which the Yankees ended up losing 14–2, Steinbrenner had shown up his soon-to-be-ex-manager by ordering the public address announcer to inform the crowd that anyone in possession of a ticket for that game would be entitled to another ticket to a future contest, free of charge.

Michael's 1981 dismissal as manager (he's a member of the Multiple Turn at the Helm Club) was particularly cute in that Steinbrenner managed to figure out a way to humiliate the skipper in front of the fans *during the game.*

You've got to give the Boss points for creativity here. He wasn't content with the standard press-conference degradation he'd already raised to unprecedented levels. He'd done the press-conference thing as well as he knew he could do it. Now he wanted something else. Steinbrenner, like any good artist, wanted to push himself to new heights.

I hate Steinbrenner . . . for misusing Yankee Stadium facilities in any number of inventive and thoroughly classless ways.

91. This Is My Ballpark, Right? Oh, It's Not?

"Steinbrenner took on his own fans when he had Yankee Stadium security guards confiscate signs saying 'George Must Go'; only an action brought by the American Civil Liberties Union prevented a recurrence."

Nope. It's not your ballpark.

As we've seen, George won a court battle defending his *own* right to criticize, publicly, those he felt didn't measure up. The right of people who *don't* happen to be millionaires to exercise the same privilege seems to be less certain in his mind. Prepare yourself for a shock: This incident seems to indicate that the big guy can dish it out, but he can't take it.

Credit where credit is due department: He *could* have fought the ACLU in court, thrown millions of dollars at a top-notch legal team, and won on some technicality. But it would have been wrong. That's for sure.

I hate Steinbrenner . . . for forever finding new ways to erode the relationship between himself and New York baseball fans after fans have concluded that things are as bad as they can possibly get. I also hate him for conveniently "forgetting" that Yankee Stadium, owned by the City of New York, is public property, and thus subject to, you know, the Bill of Rights. (Baseball *is* supposed to be the quintessentially American game, right? And actions that put a hammerlock on the Constitution *should* get the "out" signal, right?) Basically, I hate Steinbrenner for attempting to treat Yankee Stadium as though it were Steinbrennerland (when he's not threatening to vacate the premises, that is).

92. A Dizzying Series of Mystifying and/or Completely Inept Roster Moves

Forced out: Reggie Jackson, Jay Buhner, Willie McGee, Fred McGriff, Don Baylor, Dave Winfield, Jose Rijo, Doug Drabek, Jim DeShaies, Bob Tewksbury, etc., etc., etc.

Brought in: Britt Burns, Ed Whitson, Jack Clark, Danny Tartabull, Joe Niekro, Andy Hawkins, Steve Trout, Ken Phelps, Tony Fernandez, Rafael Santana, etc., etc., etc.

"Steinbrenner sucks! Steinbrenner sucks!"
   —*New York Yankees fans, en masse, on April 27, 1982, following an epic home run by California Angel (and former Yankee) Reggie Jackson. Jackson, who had been criticized and finally left to pursue*

greener pastures by the Yankee boss, later told the press, "The fans made a vocal expression that George made a mistake in letting me go. They were able to say something a little more directly than I could."

"Tell the court, Mr. Prospective Juror, do you have any strong opinions about the owner who masterminded the trade of Fred McGriff from the Yankees in exchange for a couple of no-names? Stop snarling, Prospective Juror."
—George Will.

"Baylor's bat will be dead by August."
—A widely reported Steinbrenner observation from the 1986 season. In fact, Don Baylor, traded to Boston, was a key contributor to the 1986 Boston pennant drive. The Yankees finished second behind the Red Sox in the American League East.

"Lou, I just won you the pennant. I got you Steve Trout."
—Steinbrenner's boast to Lou Piniella aside, Trout's 1987 performance for the Yankees was something less than awe inspiring, and it certainly didn't cinch the American League pennant for them. Trout got a bad case of the jitters and posted a dismal 0–4 record with a 6.60 earned-run average.

Jay Buhner for *Ken Phelps?* Man, oh man.

Jay Buhner for *Ken Phelps?* Okay, okay, I know. The 1996 Yankees benefited from some shrewd, expensive moves (rescuing Cecil Fielder from the Tigers, for instance). And now the team is basking in the glow of that long-delayed World Championship. The Boss deserves to be acknowledged for these facts. So here goes: 1996 made it all seem worthwhile. For about a week after the Series ended. And then fans started waking up in the middle of the night in a cold sweat and thinking to themselves once again. . . .

Jay Buhner for *Ken Phelps?* What was he, nuts?

I hate Steinbrenner . . . for his impulsive, idiotic player moves—a peculiarly Steinbrenner-related form of torture of which we probably have not seen the last, 1996 World Series title or no.

93. Sixty-Five and Going Strong

"Yes, today is George Steinbrenner's birthday, and the old Yankee Doodle Dandy is a sparkling 65 years old. He has spent the last 23 of those years—with time out for suspensions now and then—owning the Yankees, and that certainly is long enough to ask anyone to carry such a weighty burden."
    —*Murray Chass in the* New York Times, *July 4, 1995. Strangely, the Boss didn't take the hint.*

Could there be a mandatory retirement age for baseball owners? Not necessarily *all* baseball owners, mind you. Just the ones who happen to be, well, George Steinbrenner. Do you think we could get the commissioner's office in on this? If we ever have a commissioner's office, that is, as opposed to an *acting* commissioner's office?

Sigh. The year 1995 saw yet another opportunity for the Yankee boss to make a (relatively) graceful exit. George didn't take advantage of it. He may be waiting for everyone else to retire first. All the players. All the owners. All the umpires. All the members of the media. All the league officials. Everyone.

I hate Steinbrenner . . . for failing to retire on July 4, 1995—his 65th birthday.

94. Bus Stop (or the More Things Change . . .)

"The next time you want to go where you're not invited, check with me."
>   —*Remark on the team bus attributed to Steinbrenner after the principal owner supposedly tapped Reggie Jackson's shoulder meaningfully. The team was en route to Newark Airport during the 1996 playoffs. Jackson reportedly stood up and shouted, "I'm 50 years old—why do you treat me like you do?"*

You can always count on those trademark interpersonal skills of George's to help him launch yet another explosion at what seems like the worst possible moment. Isn't it nice to have something to rely on in this world?

Talk about your basic he-who-learns-nothing-from-history-is-condemned-to-repeat-it situation. Jackson, a Hall of Famer and perpetual fan favorite in New York, held a post as a member of

Steinbrenner's "advisory group"—but after this distracting, Stein-
brenner-induced incident summoned up memories of tabloid exploits
from postseasons past, Jackson started making noises about pulling a
Yogi, as it were, by refusing to participate in any Yankee Stadium
activity as long as Steinbrenner was on the scene.

"I'm thinking of doing what Yogi did," the *Times* quoted Jackson
as saying. "Not going back to Yankee Stadium as long as George
owns the club. Not going to Old-Timers' Day. Nothing." A Hall of
Famer and Yankee legend sounds off after having had enough of the
Boss's distinctive brand of garbage.

George brought his own unique backroom scheming and petty
jealousies to the fore at the very moment Yankees fans thought they
could relax and enjoy the playoffs. "George has been trying to break
Reggie all year," the *Times* quoted one Yankee insider as saying.
Sound familiar?

For ragging, yet again and, God knows, probably not for the last
time, on a baseball legend who's earned the right not to be screwed
around with, Steinbrenner deserves the undying enmity of baseball
fans from coast to coast.

(The two apparently ironed things out later on.)

I hate Steinbrenner . . . for dissing Reggie Jackson two decades after
Steinbrenner himself appeared to have gone about as low as it was
possible to go in that area—and for believing in his heart of hearts
that, if only he pays them, even Hall of Famers have to put up with
his abuse.

95. General Managers Can Be Quite Versatile, You Know

"Steinbrenner pulled [general manager Lou] Piniella behind a giant ficus bush. . . . 'I'm sick and tired of all these free passes being given out,' Steinbrenner said. 'There's too many people getting free passes, and I'm going to put a stop to it. Now, I want you to stay here and watch all the people who come through this gate. Count 'em and see who they are.'"
—*An unusual assignment indeed for a front-office man.*

Ever wonder why Piniella left the Yankee organization?

Whether this absurd incident was an example of Steinbrenner's sadism or his inability to view spring training matters in anything remotely resembling a realistic perspective is hard to say. George appeared to delight in playing the stimulating "Let's-torment-Lou" game. He also has been known to treat spring training games as though they were the final game of the World Series. Whatever the motivation was, this assignment makes one wonder anew about the private hell of having to report to Steinbrenner.

It could have been worse. Steinbrenner could have issued the command while compulsively shifting three small metal balls in his hand and mumbling something about stolen strawberries.

I hate Steinbrenner . . . for repeatedly demeaning, subjugating, and humiliating the people who work for him by ordering them to do outlandish things like—for instance—hide behind bushes.

96. 'Twas Right Before Christmas, and All Through the House, All the Employees Were Quaking, 'Cause George Was a Louse

"Former Yankees media relations director Rob Butcher, who[m] Steinbrenner fired last month when he left for home during the holidays, was offered his old job back. Butcher politely said no."
—*Sportswriter I. J. Rosenberg, writing in January 1996 on the* Fastball *World Wide Web site maintained by the Atlanta Braves, highlights a typical Steinbrenner human-relations tactic: act like a jerk, then try to use money to make things better afterward.*

You thought he couldn't possibly top himself, didn't you?

This is getting downright Dickensian. As the story goes, the problem was that Butcher dared to leave New York to spend some holiday time with his family—*while setting aside time to work on Yankee business from home.* Home is not where the Yankee boss's heart is, however, and there was hell to pay.

What Butcher seems to have gotten as a result of his departure was a long-distance termination a few days before St. Nick's arrival. Ho, ho, ho, everybody.

I bet the annual Christmas party was a *real* blast for Yankee employees.

Note the trademark "let's-patch-it-all-up" post-blowup attempt at reconciliation. Wonder why Butcher wouldn't take him up on it?

145

It's all a little like Ebenezer Scrooge from *A Christmas Carol*—but, see, Scrooge *changes* at the end of the story. (By the way, how much money would you pay to hear George Steinbrenner read *A Christmas Carol* out loud from beginning to end, and then discuss what he, personally, had learned from the Dickens classic?)

Actually the whole flap was motivated by the Boss's legendary generosity—a topic he never tires of talking about with reporters. You see, George was in the holiday mood, and he knew, deep in his heart, that pink slips folded into origami shapes make the very best Christmas tree decorations.

I hate Steinbrenner . . . for firing media relations director Rob Butcher shortly before Christmas.

97. Mackie Who?

"During negotiations that led to Vincent's banning Steinbrenner from baseball in 1990, Steinbrenner was asked if he was being 'Machiavellian.' He responded, [former commissioner Fay] Vincent says in the [book] proposal, by saying 'Who's he—a famous ballplayer?' "
   —*Actually, Rick Machiavelli was a backup guard for some of the great New York Knicks squads of the 1970s.*

If he didn't say it, he should have. It looks like George may have missed a superb opportunity to show off his knowledge of the classics to the commish. Tough break.

The book proposal, apparently composed by someone other than Vincent and then approved by the former commissioner for distribution to publishers, made its way to the press. At that point, in the *Times* article, Vincent distanced himself from the general tone of the book's outline, though not from its specifics. ("It's not my intention to be revengeful," he was quoted as saying. Also: "Just say I'm not writing it. You did not get the proposal legitimately.")

If the "Machiavellian" passage represents an exchange that actually took place between Vincent and Steinbrenner—and it sounded legitimate enough for the *Times* to run the story—it was definitely one of those classic Boss moments. Now it's entirely possible that we could be looking at a simple case of mistaken identity. Perhaps George, an Ohio man, was thinking of Cleveland Indians pitcher Chuck *Machemehl,* whose entire major-league career consisted of eighteen innings and an 0–2, 6.50 ERA record for the Tribe in 1971. The names *are* very similar.

Naaah.

Hey, everyone muffs a few classical references. Then again, not everyone compares himself to Patton, Lincoln, and Julius Caesar.

I hate Steinbrenner . . . because baseball's most Machiavellian owner really ought to know the meaning of the word "Machiavellian."

98. Put Up or Shut Up

"A couple of the players think I should not get involved as much as I have. They think they can do better that way, that's just fine. I'll keep the whole month of October open, anxiously awaiting the World Series at Yankee Stadium. They can put up or shut up."
  —*Excerpt from 1987 written statement released to the press.*

Notice the tantalizing rhetorical flourish—"They think they can do better that way, that's just fine"—which seems to leave open the possibility that, under some vaguely defined set of circumstances, George might not get involved quite as much as he has.

George may have been hoping to earn brownie points for his discreet decision not to name the individual players who were tired of his endless, borderline-clinical self-aggrandizement. Or he may have been hoping just to save time, since reading off all the names on that list would have taken a while.

Now here's the big question. The Yankees finally won the World Series again in 1996, for which we thank the baseball gods ten thousand times. Now that his team has put up, can we call George on the debt—and expect him to leave all, and I do mean all, major decisions concerning personnel and on-field strategy to his manager and general manager?

Hmmmmm?

I hate Steinbrenner . . . for hinting at promises he never intended to keep and for subjecting unnamed members of his own team to public abuse.

99. Live, From New York, It's George Steinbrenner

Be honest. Wasn't the Boss's appearance on *Saturday Night Live* a real travesty?

Here are five random observations from outsiders about the Boss. Look them over and see if you don't agree that any *one* of them is far, far funnier than George's entire guest-host performance.

"It's a beautiful thing to behold, with all 36 oars working in unison."
—*Announcer Jack Buck, on George Steinbrenner's yacht.*

"Nothing is more limited than being a limited partner of George's."
—*Steinbrenner's erstwhile business associate John McMullen.*

"I think his being kicked out of baseball is really bad for American business and human relations, because we have now lost a symbol of how not to do things."
—*Jim Bouton, commenting to the press on Steinbrenner's short-lived 1990 banishment from the game.*

"Sooner or later, of course, being the apple of [George Steinbrenner's] eye is the same as being the apple of William Tell's eye."
—*Sportswriter Dave Anderson on reports that a particular managerial candidate was "the apple of George Steinbrenner's eye."*

"George is the guy with the boats. One of them is the *Titanic*."
—*Earl Weaver during the 1980 pennant race.*

I rest my case.

I hate Steinbrenner . . . for failing to live up to his true comic potential on *Saturday Night Live* (and *Seinfeld*, for that matter).

100. The Inevitable Next Outrage, The Inevitable Next Comeback

"At Yankee Stadium, where the last-place club that Steinbrenner has assembled (a Mercenaries Row of no-talent free agents, high-priced castoffs, and rookies) was playing the Detroit Tigers, the crowd rose in a standing ovation when the news spread that the familiar chant 'the Boss must go' would actually become a reality."
—*And yet, like a bad penny, the Boss was back in the spring of 1993.*

Open hostility from the paying customers. Trouble with commissioners. Trouble with managers. Trouble with players. Trouble with a gambler. Not one but two heave-hos. Headline-making trouble with

Reggie Jackson *all over again* in 1996. And the man just keeps coming back. As these words are being written, George Steinbrenner sits once again at the top of the baseball world.

What will it take to make him go away and *stay* gone? When will the day finally come that Steinbrenner focuses on boats—or anything else—rather than baseball?

Maybe never. Try this simple experiment. Go to the library. Ask the reference librarian to point you toward the biggest encyclopedia in the building. Open it up and find the heading for "Inability to Take Hints From the Rest of the Country." There you may see a photograph of a battle-scarred former President of the United States who, even after having made his share of "mistakes" during the "Watergate period," and even after having gone down in history as the least popular politician in the long and tumultuous history of our republic, managed somehow, in his later years, to emerge as a respected elder statesman.

The reader will forgive me for noting once again that George Steinbrenner was a strong supporter of this man. We haven't been able to focus in on this fact in this book quite as much as I might like, because there's been a whole lot of other stuff to talk about. It is nevertheless the case. Steinbrenner was a big Nixon fan during Tricky Dick's heyday. (Sometimes, of course, it seems as though, in the ultimate rebuke to his detractors, the Master of San Clemente saved his last and most impressive comeback for the period directly following his death, which would make *this* his heyday. But I digress.)

For all anyone knows, Steinbrenner may still consider the thirty-seventh president a preeminent role model, more compelling in his life's example than Lincoln or Patton or Julius Caesar or anyone else. If there isn't a framed photo of Nixon on the Boss's desk, ready to be gazed at for inspiration after the fallout from the most recent misguided Steinbrenner explosion, there really ought to be. Because both men had a way of coming back when you were really, really sick of them.

A recent (and thoroughly unscientific) Internet poll about Steinbrenner prompted one fan of the Bronx Bombers to ask, "How can you be a Yankee fan and not hate him?" This while the team was leading the American League East and rumbling toward its first world championship since 1978. But fan discontent or no fan discontent, George is on record as having maintained that the New York Yankees represent "something you never sell." No matter what the fans have to say, it looks like they'll have Steinbrenner to kick around for a while.

Which means we can all take a deep breath and get ready for the next Outrageous Stunt from Steinbrenner. The man's at the top of his game, and a fair number of Yankees fans are luxuriating in the glow of the '96 squad, wondering if perhaps, just perhaps, they've been too hard on the Boss over the years. Yeah, right. Make no mistake. The stage is set. We can all rest assured that the next fiasco probably won't be long in coming at all.

I hate Steinbrenner . . . for ignoring the wishes of Yankees fans and staying on as principal Yankee owner for the foreseeable future.

101. Thank God for Joe Torre ... but You Can't Help Wondering ...

Will he last? After the Yankees lost Game One of the 1996 Series against the Braves, the Boss came barging into manager Torre's office and started to launch his patented you'd-better-deliver-or-there's-gonna-be-trouble speech. It's a speech he's delivered on countless occasions to countless managers, usually—not always, but usually—with less than exemplary results. This time it began with a sage pronouncement about Game Two: "This is a must win!"

Some managers would have responded to the tirade by saying absolutely nothing.

Some managers would have responded to this classic Steinbrenner tirade by acknowledging the must-win status of the situation, nodding attentively, agreeing whenever appropriate and waiting for the boss to stop talking. (Alas, it sometimes takes a while.)

Some managers would have responded to Steinbrenner's theatrics by thanking him for his intuitive grasp of the obvious and informing him that lecturing competent professionals about how they have to avoid losing two straight World Series games at home is, well, a little counterproductive.

Joe Torre may be the first manager to respond to George's tablepounding by confronting it head on.

"Hey, we'll probably lose tonight, too, George," Torre responded glibly before Game Two. "But Atlanta's my home town. We'll sweep them there and win it back home." That, according to *Sports Illus-*

trated, was Torre's response to the vexing managerial challenge Yankees fans thought would never be resolved. When the Boss starts to play Let's Overpressure the Manager (or, if you prefer, Let's Start Focusing on Head Games So We Can Blow the 1996 World Series), *call his bluff*. Say you think the sky really *is* going to fall. Then outline a plan and pray he leaves you alone for a few moments at a stretch so you can do the job you were supposedly hired to do.

Bless Joe Torre's heart, that appears to be exactly what he did. May he and everyone else in the Yankee organization continue to confront the Boss—and deliver the results over which the Boss hyperventilates so needlessly and counterproductively—until George either changes his spots or sells the team to someone who knows how to back off.

Who'd Have Thunk It Department: When you let people who know what they're doing call the shots, some wondrous things can happen.

I hate Steinbrenner . . . because he doesn't always have managers like Torre who will call him on his b.s.—and if history is any guide, he'll find some reason to get rid of Torre eventually too. All the same, let's say a quiet, totally irrational closing prayer here, and ask that the Almighty will see fit to persuade the Boss to change his ways . . . allow Torre to stick around for a while . . . and, who knows, maybe even *lighten up and enjoy owning the New York Yankees for a change.*

Epilogue—Recalling the Roots of the New Beginning (A Satirical Fantasia)

JUNE 1, 2010

Sure, things are great for the Yankees—now. They've established their Second Great Dynasty, and they've got yet another double-digit lead in games over the hapless Boston Red Sox. They seem perfectly poised to cruise to the World Series yet again—and who knows? They may just make good on that public promise they made to their kindly, gray-haired owner in the locker room at the end of last season, after they defeated the Mexico City Caballeros in the World Series. They may just capture their twelfth consecutive Series trophy in 2010 . . . and snag their fourteenth pennant in the past fifteen years.

If they do, it will be for one simple reason. These players *love* their owner.

George Steinbrenner, of course, is revered as no owner in all of big-league ball. But—and we tend to forget this—it was not always thus.

Think back to the very beginnings of the Second Great Dynasty— if you're old enough to remember 1996 clearly, that is. Think back to how Steinbrenner turned everything around shortly after that extraordinary, epoch-launching New York Yankees World Championship season of 1996. Take a moment to remind yourself he took everyone in organized baseball by surprise and reclaimed the long-tarnished Yankee legacy with the now-famous Five Yankee Reforms program.

You must remember how it all started. Steinbrenner announced, shortly after spring training in 1997, that he was scaling back the hefty ticket increases he'd been talking about instituting at Yankee Stadium. In fact he went even further—he rolled ticket prices back to their *1978* levels in honor of the miracle World Championship of that historic season. Amazed fans responded by selling out 95 percent of all Yankee Stadium regular-season games that season . . . and every season since. No one, including Steinbrenner, knew it then, but the rollbacks marked the first of the five organizational reforms that made the Second Great Dynasty possible. Other fan-friendly initiatives followed in short order as part of this first Reform. Remember the Revive the Yankee Stadium Neighborhood Zone Fund, to which Steinbrenner personally contributed over $20 million? Or how about the special Kids Schedule for playoff games—so relentlessly lobbied for by Steinbrenner in the face of network opposition—that permitted 3:00 P.M. starts for selected postseason contests? In the end it was Steinbrenner's own (expensive) live television appeal during a one-hour infomercial that finally generated enough public outrage over the postmidnight finishes of key October games to force the networks to make the change. Could a single sentence from the Yankee owner have been what turned the tide? George's now-famous summation of the problem came close: "Ratings and broadcast revenue be damned—if there aren't any kids watching the playoff games now, there won't be any *grownups* watching any games tomorrow!"

Then, in 1998, the second of the Reforms kicked in. Manager Joe Torre, the skipper of the triumphant 1996 squad, found himself guiding a battered, bewildered Yankee club through a tough year . . . and, on the final day of the season, looking at a disappointing Bronx Bomber finish in the American League East. Of course, Steinbrenner summoned Torre to his office for a much-publicized heart-to-heart talk. Yankee fans steeled themselves for the news that Torre, like so many managers before him, would be canned. In fact Steinbrenner signed the miracle worker of '96 to a seven-year deal . . . via an agreement that granted the manager 85 percent of all Steinbrenner's *personal* assets if the Boss decided, for any reason, to dismiss his manager ahead of time. "There's been enough bloodletting in the past," Steinbrenner was quoted as saying in early 1999. "I wanted to give Joe—and the fans of New York—a clear indication that there would be some stability in the dugout for the foreseeable future." George was as good as his word, and he later vowed to make this personal-assets feature an element of all his future contracts with managers. The second of the Five Reforms—The Managerial Stability Clause, it was called—was an even better public-relations move than the first. And it led Torre and the Yankees to a string of pennants and World Series trophies. "When the players know who's in charge," Steinbrenner observed in April of the year 2000, "and when that person is the manager, and when the players know, in their heart of hearts, that the manager is going to stick around for a while and be rewarded for good work, then the on-field play gets a whole lot better. I can't believe I never realized that before. But I'm going to go out of my way to let everyone in baseball know that I sure realize it now."

The third of the five Reforms, of course, was the Front-Office Stability Pact. Hirings and firings at Yankee Stadium quickly became the rarest of all news events. It seems impossible to believe now, but the Yankee organization was once known as a place of turmoil, paranoia, heartache, betrayal, and low morale. Under Steinbrenner's leadership during the Second Great Dynasty, of course, job security at Yankee Stadium is at an all-time high.

Steinbrenner wasn't satisfied with just three ground-breaking reform efforts, however. He knew that if the Yankees were to remain stable, profitable, and successful for a prolonged period, he'd have to let his players know, on a regular basis, how much he appreciated their efforts. That's why he launched his trademark "What I Love About the New York Yankees" column, a weekly piece George has *paid* to have appear in the New York dailies regularly for the past twelve years. It may come as a surprise to many readers of George's column nowadays, but the genial old Boss was once highly and loudly critical of certain Yankee players. With the imposition of the fourth Reform, under which Steinbrenner has pledged never to publicly (or privately, for that matter) criticize any player in pinstripes, those memories seem far away indeed.

The fifth (and final) Reform was the one that proved most shocking to long-term Yankee fans. But those fans who knew the real George Steinbrenner saw it coming back in the mid-to-late nineties. Steinbrenner himself put it this way in a 2004 interview with *Yankee Doodle* magazine—the popular house newsletter of the high-morale, high-continuity, high-commitment organization: "Without a full-time independent commissioner, major-league baseball was a farce. I knew it, the other owners knew it, the broadcasters knew it, and, worst of all, the fans knew it. Everyone knew that the whole idea behind the commissioner's office when it was originally set up had been to help prevent excesses and keep an eye out for the long-term interests of the game in a way that no other official can. I lost sight of that role for a while, but hey, you live and you learn. With age, one hopes, comes maturity and a little greater insight, a little greater wisdom. I saw the error of my ways. So that's why, in early 2003, I began to lobby the other owners to rename Fay Vincent as the permanent, full-time commissioner of baseball once again. Since he's come back on board, Fay has helped us to get the game back on the right footing for a new century, and we're all deeply grateful for his help in guiding the owners and telling us all when we're off the mark as far as the long-term interests of the game are concerned. Letting him go was a huge mistake, and we all realize that now." Steinbrenner's successful efforts to reinstate Vincent—the Fifth of the major reforms—paved the way for a new Golden Era for the Yankees as a franchise and for big-league baseball as a whole.

As a result of these actions, and many others too numerous to detail here, Steinbrenner put the Yankees back where they belonged: at the top of a stable baseball world. He emerged as the respected, responsible, elder statesman of the game of baseball, a role that few who followed his tenure as owner would ever have predicted for him—but one that today's Yankee fans know full well is a role he was destined to play.

As the faithful look forward expectantly to even greater triumphs from the 2010 season, it's good to remember that the Second

Great Dynasty didn't just *happen*. It came about as the result of the conscious choices of a single beloved and inspired baseball executive, a man whose place in the Hall of Fame seems now like a foregone conclusion.

There was a time, amazingly enough, when people believed George Steinbrenner incapable of such deeds. There was a time when Steinbrenner inspired fear and loathing among the Yankee faithful, rather than adulation and the deepest respect for his many accomplishments as a wise, retiring leader of men. There was a time when Steinbrenner was thought to be among the most spiteful, incompetent, and self-aggrandizing figures in all of sport. But that time is no more. And why? Because George Steinbrenner knew how to turn things around.

When asked recently about the secret of his success, the kindly, avuncular elderly figure Yankee fans have grown to love above all but a handful of others had a simple, eloquent response. "The key to leaving a positive impression in this crazy world of ours," Steinbrenner confided to one former critic in August of 2008, "is the ability to take constructive advice in stride and react gracefully to it. That's the only secret I have to pass along."

Words to live by.

Notes

The sources of the quotes not fully cited in the text are as follows:

PAGE

xxii	*Chass*	*New York Times Magazine*, March 28, 1993.
2	*CBS sale*	Dick Schaap, *Steinbrenner!*, New York: G. P. Putnam's Sons, 1982, p. 110.
6	*Shipping company bailout*	Donald Dewey and Nicholas Acocella, *The Encyclopedia of Major League Baseball Teams*, New York: HarperCollins, p. 384.
11	On *Cap position*	Robert Obojski, *Baseball's Strangest Moments*, New York: Sterling Publishing, 1988, p. 57.
12	*Berkow*	*New York Times*, August 18, 1991.
	Chass	*New York Times*, August 16, 1991.
	Curry	*New York Times*, August 18, 1991.
	Chass	*New York Times*, August 16, 1991.
14	On *Doyle Alexander*	Bill Madden and Moss Klein, *Damned Yankees*, New York: Warner Books, 1990, p. 5.
16	On *Winfield/Spira*	Dewey and Acocella, op. cit., p. 383.
18	On *Beattie*	This quote appeared in various news reports in early 1978.

18	On *Griffin*	Kevin Nelson, *Baseball's Even Greater Insults*, New York: Fireside Books, 1993, p. 122.
	On *Rasmussen*	Murray Chass, *New York Times*, July 4, 1995
22	*Jackson remarks on Rosen*	Maury Allen, *Mr. October*, New York: Times Books, 1981, p. 214.
23	*Martin story*	Dick Schaap, *Steinbrenner!*, New York: G. Putnam's Sons, 1982, p. 168.
24	On *Piniella*	Kevin Nelson, *Baseball's Even Greater Insults*, New York: Fireside, 1993, p. 125.
25	*Eye tests*	Dave Winfield and Tom Parker, *Winfield: A Player's Life*, New York: Avon Books, 1989, p. 151.
27	On *Strawberry*	NBC Sports World Wide Web site, accessed October 8, 1996.
28	On *Nettles's weight*	This quote was widely circulated through various media outlets during 1980 and in following seasons.
	"I'd take him back . . ."	Bill Madden and Moss Klein, *Damned Yankees*, New York: Warner Books, 1990, p. 155.
	"Reggie isn't . . ."	Allen, op. cit., p. 238.
29	*"Winfield's a good . . ."*	This quote appeared in various news reports in early 1982.
31	*"(O)ut of the goodness . . ."*	David A. Kaplan et al., *Newsweek*, August 6, 1990.
32	*"My son Hank . . . "*	August 1990 press statement.
34	*Struggle over Yankee home field*	Peter Grant, *New York Daily News*, October 5, 1995.
35	*Advantages of power*	Schaap, op. cit., p. 302.

40	*Murray story*	Bowie Kuhn, *Hardball: The Education of a Baseball Commissioner,* New York: Times Books, 1987, p. 209.
41	*Selig story*	*Boston Globe* editorial, September 18, 1994.
46	*Response to Cerone*	Schaap, op. cit., p. 273.
48	*Call to Erra*	Winfield and Parker, op. cit., p. 134.
49	*Murcer error*	Obojski, op. cit., p. 58.
	Remark to Martin	Madden and Klein, op. cit., p.15.
52	*Nettles on plane travel*	Dewey and Acocella, op. cit., p. 380.
53	*Call to dugout*	Schaap, op. cit., p. 202.
54	*Call to training room*	Winfield and Parker, op. cit., p. 250.
55	*"You think this is funny?"*	Madden and Klein, op. cit., p. 58.
56	*Discussion with Frohman*	Winfield and Parker, op. cit., p. 142.
58	*Winfield in '92 Series*	David Nemec, *Great Baseball Feats, Facts, and Firsts,* New York: Signet, 1990, p. 407.
59	On *umpires*	Joel Zoss and John Bowman, *Diamonds in the Rough,* Chicago: Contemporary, 1996, p. 298.
65	*Roy Cohn*	Winfield and Parker, op. cit., p. 181.
66	*CDAB* entry	John S. Bowman, ed., *Cambridge Dictionary of American Biography,* New York: Cambridge University Press, 1995.
68	*Hands-on management*	David H. Nathan, *Baseball Quotations,* New York: Ballantine Books, 1991, p. 80.

69	*Infielder's error*	Nelson, op. cit., p. 121.
70	*Ferraro signal*	Ibid., p. 122.
71	*Ice chunks*	Schaap, op. cit., p. 260.
72	*Morale at American Ship*	Kaplan et al., op. cit.
	Switchboard operator	Obojski, op. cit., p. 58.
74	*"Oh, no you don't . . ."*	Madden and Klein, op. cit., p. 81.
75	*Red lips*	Schaap, op. cit., p. 262.
76	On *free agency*	Mike Shatzkin, *The Ballplayers,* New York: Arbor House, William Morrow, 1990, p. 104.
78	*"I have not been there . . ."*	Murray Chass, *New York Times Magazine,* March 28, 1993.
79	*Community relations*	Juan Forero, *New York Newsday,* July 10, 1994.
80	On *Gabe Paul*	Murray Chass, *New York Times,* July 4, 1995.
83	*Kubek's appeal*	Steve Zipay, *New York Newsday,* July 1, 1994.
85	*Replacement players*	Pete Bowles and Steve Zipay, *New York Newsday,* March 18, 1995.
86	*Jackson's suite*	Allen, op. cit., p. 210.
	Behavior in Yankee Stadium Box	Kuhn, op. cit., p. 209.
	Sandwich episode	Murray Chass, *New York Times,* July 4, 1995.
87	*Plane reservation episode*	Kaplan et al., op. cit.
	Tax form episode	Murray Chass, *New York Times,* July 4, 1995.

88	On *coaches*	Nelson, op. cit., p. 127.
89	On *Michael and Showalter*	Dave Anderson, *New York Times,* October 28, 1995.
91	*Dealings with subordinates*	George Vecsey, *New York Times,* October 27, 1995.
92	*Martin telegram*	Schaap, op. cit., p. 295.
99	*Second-guessing*	Madden and Klein, op. cit., p. 119.
100	*Landmarks*	Murray Chass, *New York Times,* June 6, 1995.
103	*Topless bar incident*	Madden and Klein, op. cit., p. 9.
107	*Lemon pledge*	Schaap, op. cit., p. 308.
108	*Michael protests*	Madden and Klein, op. cit., p. 52.
109	*Berra pledge*	Nathan, op. cit., p. 52.
	Berra reversal	Madden and Klein, op. cit., p. 60.
	Berra's boycott	Murray Chass, *New York Times,* June 6, 1995.
113	*Hernia sign*	Kaplan et al., op. cit.
118	*Mixed signals on Showalter departure*	Murray Chass, *New York Times,* October 27, 1995.
119	*Criticism of Buck*	Ibid.
121	*Showalter reversal*	Jack Curry, *New York Times,* December 3, 1995.
123	*Julius Caesar*	Nathan, op. cit., p. 170.
125	*Abraham Lincoln*	Kaplan et al., op. cit.
126	*Admiral reference*	Winfield and Parker, op. cit., p. 203.
127	*George S. Patton*	Kaplan et al., op. cit.

128	*Exaggerated homerun swing*	Obojski, op. cit., p. 56.
129	On *Winfield*	Nelson, op. cit., p. 122.
130	*Luxury boxes*	*Boston Globe*, December 22, 1994.
131	*Land ownership*	Nathan, op. cit., p. 81.
	Pep talks	Schaap, op. cit., p. 167.
132	*Jackson's bossiness*	Schaap, op. cit., p. 281.
	Bills	Nelson, op. cit., p. 123.
133	*Court hours*	Winfield and Parker, op. cit., p. 185.
	On *Gabe Paul*	Murray Chass, *New York Times*, July 4, 1995.
	Admiral reference	Winfield and Parker, op. cit., p. 201.
	Hard on close people	Ibid., p. 202.
	Winning	Kaplan et al., op. cit.
	Leadership	Claire Smith, *New York Times*, June 5, 1995.
134	*Confiscated bat episode*	*New York Times*, June 6, 1995.
137	*ACLU incident*	Dewey and Acocella, op. cit., p. 382.
139	*McGriff trade*	George Will, *Newsweek*, August 6, 1990.
	Steve Trout	Madden and Klein, op. cit., p. 95.
141	*Bus incident*	*New York Times*, October 8, 1996, p. 167.
143	*Ficus bush incident*	Madden and Klein, op. cit., p. 183.
146	*Machiavelli remark*	*New York Times*, March 4, 1994.
149	*Yacht remark*	Nathan, op. cit., p. 216.

149	On *limited partnership*	Shatzkin, op. cit., p. 104.
	Bouton quote	Nathan, op. cit., p. 170.
150	*Anderson quote*	Nathan, op. cit., p. 170.
	Weaver quote	Allen, op. cit., p. 239.
	"Boss must go"	Walter Shapiro, *Time,* August 13, 1990.

Acknowledgments

Among the many people who helped make this book a reality: my editor, Jim Ellison, whose patience, support, and inspired guidance is much appreciated, as always; my agent, Bert Holtje; my friend, Glenn KnicKrehm, without whom *no* Beach Brook production would ever have come into existence; Mark Wallstein, my dear friend; Bob and Leslie Tragert, who were always there with ideas and moral support; Henry and Mary Tragert, providers of my writing cabin; and the beloved members of my immediate family, Mary Toropov (my ever-patient wife), Judith Burros (my ever-patient mother), and David, Stephen, and Julia Toropov (my ever-patient children).

About the Author

Brandon Toropov is a Boston-based writer whose other books include *Fifty Biggest Baseball Myths* (Citadel Press) and *Who Was Eleanor Rigby . . . and 908 More Questions and Answers About the Beatles.*